YOUR r
could ap
in our r
cookbook!

Share your tried & true family favorites with us instantly at
www.gooseberrypatch.com
If you'd rather jot 'em down by hand, just mail this form to...
Gooseberry Patch • Cookbooks – Call for Recipes
2500 Farmers Dr., #110 • Columbus, OH 43235

If your recipe is selected for a book, you'll receive a FREE copy!

Please share only your original recipes or those that you have made your own over the years.

Recipe Name:

Number of Servings:

Any fond memories about this recipe? Special touches you like to add
or handy shortcuts?

Ingredients (include specific measurements):

Instructions (continue on back if needed):

Special Code: **Garfield**

Over ➶

Extra space for recipe if needed:

Tell us about yourself...

Your complete contact information is needed so that we can send you your FREE cookbook, if your recipe is published. Phone numbers and email addresses are kept private and will only be used if we have questions about your recipe.

Name:
Address:
City: State: Zip:
Email:
Daytime Phone:

Thank you! Vickie & JoAnn

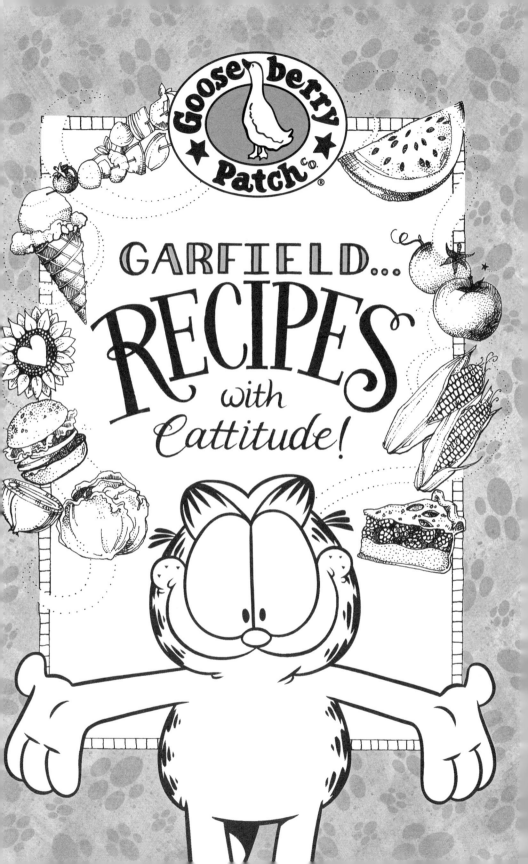

Gooseberry Patch
2500 Farmers Dr., #110
Columbus, OH 43235

www.gooseberrypatch.com
1·800·854·6673

Do you have a tried & true recipe...
tip, craft or memory that you'd like to see featured in a **Gooseberry
Patch** cookbook? Visit our website at **www.gooseberrypatch.com**
to share them with us instantly. If you'd rather jot them down by hand,
use the handy form in the front of this book and send them to...

Gooseberry Patch
Attn: Cookbook Dept.
2500 Farmers Dr., #110
Columbus, OH 43235

Don't forget to include the number of servings your recipe makes,
plus your name, address, phone number and email address.
If we select your recipe, your name will appear right along
with it...and you'll receive a **FREE** copy of the cookbook!

Contents

Dedication

TO FANS OF GOOSEBERRY PATCH AND
GARFIELD EVERYWHERE...BROUGHT
TOGETHER BY A COMMON LOVE OF
YUMMY HOMESTYLE FOOD!

Breakfast Is Served...
Time to Get Up!

Cold pizza and orange juice... the best breakfast ever!

BREAKFAST IS SERVED...
TIME TO GET UP!

Creamy Scrambled Eggs & Chives

Eggs are delicious with herbs...try dill weed, thyme and parsley too.
No catnip, unless Garfield is coming for breakfast!

8 eggs	1/4 t. pepper
1/4 c. water	2 to 3 t. butter
2 T. fresh chives, chopped	1/2 c. cream cheese, cubed
1/2 t. salt	

Combine eggs, water, chives, salt and pepper in a bowl. Whisk well and set aside. Melt butter in a skillet over medium-low heat; pour in egg mixture. As eggs begin to set, push them gently toward center with a spatula so that uncooked egg can flow toward sides of skillet. When eggs are partially set, add cream cheese. Continue cooking for one more minute, stirring occasionally, or until eggs are set but still moist. Makes 4 servings.

Eating breakfast on the run? Scrambled eggs turn into a portable breakfast when spooned into a pita half.

Crustless Breakfast Pie

A wonderful way to use up last night's leftover potatoes and ham.
Sliced mushrooms and chopped tomato would be tasty too.

2 c. cooked potatoes, diced
1 to 2 T. butter
1/2 c. onion, chopped
1/2 c. red or green pepper,
   chopped

2/3 c. cooked ham or crisply
   cooked bacon, diced
salt and pepper to taste
4 eggs, beaten
2 T. milk

In a skillet over medium heat, cook potatoes in butter until golden,
5 to 6 minutes. Add onion and red or green pepper; cook until onion is
translucent, about 5 minutes. Remove skillet from heat; stir in ham or
bacon, salt and pepper. Spoon potato mixture into a lightly greased
9" pie plate. In a small bowl, whisk together eggs and milk. Pour
egg mixture over potato mixture. Bake at 350 degrees for 12 to
15 minutes, until eggs are set and center tests clean with a knife tip.
Cut into wedges. Makes 4 to 6 servings.

Butter-flavored non-stick vegetable spray is handy at
breakfast time. Spritz it on a skillet, waffle iron or
pancake griddle in a jiffy. You'll even save calories
by using it instead of butter or oil!

BREAKFAST IS SERVED... TIME TO GET UP!

Morning Egg Mix-Up

A hearty breakfast in no time! Frozen diced potatoes are speedy in this recipe...there's no need to thaw them first.

2 T. oil
2 c. frozen diced potatoes
1 c. cooked ham, diced
1/2 c. onion, chopped

6 eggs, beaten
salt and pepper to taste
1 c. shredded Cheddar cheese

Heat oil in a large skillet over medium heat; add potatoes, ham and onion. Cook for 10 minutes, stirring occasionally, or until potatoes are tender. In a bowl, whisk together eggs, salt and pepper. Reduce heat to low; add eggs to skillet. Cook, stirring occasionally, until eggs are set. Remove skillet from heat; gently stir in cheese. Let stand for a few minutes, until cheese is melted. Serves 4.

Love cheesy scrambled eggs, overstuffed omelets and other egg dishes, but you're always too sleepy or short on time to fix them for breakfast? Good news... they're yummy at dinnertime too!

Cheese & Onion Omelet

No tricky flipping required with this easy method! Fill your omelet with extra cooked veggies or meat too, just warm them first.

2 T. onion, chopped
2 to 3 t. olive oil, divided
2 eggs, beaten
1 T. sour cream
1/4 t. onion powder

1/8 t. nutmeg
salt and pepper to taste
1/4 c. shredded Parmesan
   cheese

In a skillet over medium heat, sauté onion in 2 teaspoons oil until translucent. In a bowl, whisk together eggs, sour cream and seasonings. Add a little more oil to skillet, if needed; reduce heat to low. Pour egg mixture into skillet; swirl eggs around to fill skillet. Cook without stirring for 2 to 3 minutes, until eggs are lightly cooked through. Add cheese to one side of skillet; fold over omelet with a spatula. Let stand for a few minutes, until cheese melts. Serves one.

Don't work too hard cleaning up after breakfast!
To remove egg from bowls and pans, soak them in
cold water, not hot. Hot water actually cooks the egg,
making it more difficult to scrub off.

BREAKFAST IS SERVED...
TIME TO GET UP!

Egg in a Nest

Our favorite orange cat is partial to robin and sparrow eggs...
but we suggest you stick to the chicken kind!

3 to 4 T. butter, softened and
  divided
4 slices white or whole-wheat
  bread

4 eggs
salt and pepper to taste

Spread one tablespoon of butter lightly over both sides of bread slices.
Cut a hole in the center of each slice with a biscuit cutter or a small
juice glass. Add remaining butter to a skillet over medium-low heat.
Cook bread slices for 2 minutes on each side, or until toasty and
golden. Break an egg into each hole. Cook for another 2 to 3 minutes,
until eggs are lightly set on top. Season with salt and pepper. Carefully
turn with a spatula; cook on other side for one to 2 minutes, to desired
doneness. Circles may be toasted in the skillet and served alongside the
bread. Makes 4 servings.

Homestyle Potato Pancakes

There's no more delectable way to enjoy leftover
mashed potatoes! Top with sour cream...mmm.

2 eggs, beaten
4 c. mashed potatoes
2 onions, finely chopped

1 t. salt
1/2 t. pepper
1/4 c. olive oil

Combine all ingredients except oil in a bowl; stir well to blend. Heat
oil in a large skillet over medium heat. Drop potato mixture into oil by
1/4 cupfuls; flatten each to 3/4-inch thick with a spatula. Cook until
golden on both sides. Makes 6 servings.

Eggs and potatoes are tasty with catsup, but to really
wake yourself up at breakfast, add some spicy salsa!

Cheesy Scramblin' Pizza

Cold pizza and orange juice for breakfast...what could be better?
A warm egg pizza, that's what! Even Garfield would
scramble out of bed for this!

6 eggs, beaten
1/4 c. milk
1/4 c. green onions, sliced
1 tomato, chopped
12-inch pre-baked Italian
   pizza crust

8-oz. pkg. pasteurized processed
   cheese spread, cubed
6 slices bacon, cut into 1-inch
   pieces and crisply cooked

In a bowl, whisk together eggs, milk, onions and tomato; pour into a skillet sprayed with non-stick vegetable spray. Cook over low heat until eggs are set, stirring occasionally. Remove from heat. Place pizza crust on an ungreased baking sheet. Top with egg mixture, cheese and bacon. Bake at 450 degrees for 10 minutes, or until cheese is melted. Cut into wedges. Serves 6.

Breakfast Burritos

Wrap these tasty burritos in foil to freeze for later.
Unwrap and warm 'em up in the microwave.

16-oz. pkg. hot or mild ground
   pork breakfast sausage
8-oz. pkg. shredded Mexican-
   blend cheese

10-oz. can diced tomatoes with
   green chiles, drained
5 eggs, beaten
8 10-inch flour tortillas

Brown sausage in a skillet over medium heat; drain. Combine sausage, cheese and tomatoes in a bowl; set aside. Add eggs to skillet; cook over low heat until set, stirring occasionally. Add eggs to sausage mixture; mix well. Divide mixture evenly among tortillas and roll up tightly. To seal, cook burritos, seam-side down, for one to 2 minutes on a lightly greased hot griddle. Makes 8 servings.

Sunny-Side Up Breakfast Egg Pizza

*Chop up everything the night before and tuck it
in the fridge. In the morning, your breakfast pizza
will be delivered quick as a wink!*

12-inch pre-baked Italian
   pizza crust
6 eggs
salt and pepper to taste
8 slices bacon, crisply cooked
   and crumbled

1 c. red and/or green pepper,
   diced
1 onion, diced
1-1/2 c. shredded mozzarella
   cheese

Place pizza crust on an ungreased 12" round pizza pan. With a biscuit
cutter or small juice glass, cut 6 circles out of crust, evenly spaced and
about one inch from the edge. Reserve crust circles for another use.
Break an egg into each hole; season with salt and pepper. Top crust
with bacon, peppers, onion and cheese. Bake at 450 degrees for 8 to
10 minutes, until eggs are completely set. Slice into wedges, with
one egg per wedge. Makes 6 servings.

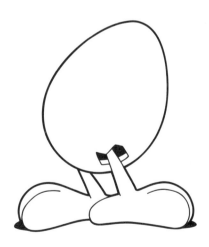

Fresh eggs can safely be kept in the refrigerator
for 4 to 5 weeks...go ahead and stock up when
they're on sale.

Farmhouse Sausage Patties

Taste-test the seasoning by frying a small patty of the freshly mixed sausage. Like it spicy? Add a sprinkle of cayenne pepper.

1 lb. ground pork
1 t. ground cumin
1/2 t. dried thyme
1/2 t. dried sage

1 t. salt
1/2 t. pepper
Optional: 1/8 t. cayenne pepper

Combine all ingredients in a bowl; mix well with your hands. Cover and refrigerate overnight to allow flavors to blend. Form into 6 to 8 patties. Arrange patties in a lightly greased skillet over medium heat. Cook until browned on both sides; drain. Serves 6 to 8.

Country Sausage Gravy

For delicious homemade biscuits, check out the recipe on page 51.

1 lb. ground pork breakfast
    sausage
12-oz. can evaporated milk
1/4 c. butter, softened

2 to 3 T. all-purpose flour
garlic salt and pepper to taste
6 buttermilk biscuits, split

Brown sausage in a skillet over medium heat; partially drain. Stir in milk; bring to a low simmer. In a small bowl, blend together butter and flour until smooth; slowly stir into sausage mixture. Add seasonings. Cook over low heat for 5 minutes, stirring frequently, or until thickened. Spoon gravy over warm biscuits. Serves 6.

Gather clothes, keys and other important stuff before you go to bed so the morning routine doesn't turn into a mad rush. More time to enjoy breakfast!

Crispy Home Fries

What's better than golden home fries? Home fries made with two kinds of potatoes!

2 lbs. Yukon Gold potatoes, peeled and cubed
2 lbs. sweet potatoes, peeled and cubed
3 T. butter

1 onion, coarsely chopped
2 cloves garlic, minced
3/4 t. salt
1/2 t. pepper

Place Yukon Gold potatoes in a large saucepan; cover with water. Bring to a boil over high heat. Boil for 2 minutes; add sweet potatoes. Return to a boil. Cook for 10 to 12 minutes, until potatoes are tender. Drain; let cool. Meanwhile, melt butter in a large skillet over medium heat. Add onion; cook for 5 to 7 minutes, until softened. Add garlic; cook for one minute. Add potatoes, salt and pepper. Cook for 15 to 20 minutes, stirring occasionally, until golden. Makes 8 servings.

Eggs to order! For eggs sunny-side up, break two or three eggs into a buttered skillet over medium-low heat. Cook until the edges begin to set, then pour in a tablespoon of water. Cover skillet and turn up the heat a little. Cook for one to two minutes more, until yolks are as done as you like. For eggs over easy, carefully turn the eggs over when the edges set, and finish cooking the same way.

Scrambled Eggs in Toast Cups

Mmm...eggs you can eat with your hands! When friends come for brunch, these cute little toast cups look nice on a platter.

5 thin slices white bread, crusts trimmed
1 T. butter, softened and divided
2 eggs, beaten
2 T. milk
salt and pepper to taste

1/2 c. cooked ham, diced
3 T. canned mushrooms, chopped
1/3 c. shredded Cheddar cheese, divided

Spread bread slices on both sides with half of the butter. Gently press each slice into a buttered muffin cup. Bake at 375 degrees for 3 minutes, or until lightly toasted; remove from oven. In a bowl, whisk together eggs, milk, salt and pepper. Add ham, mushrooms and 2 tablespoons cheese; mix well. Melt remaining butter in a skillet over medium-low heat. Pour in egg mixture; cook and stir until eggs are barely set. Spoon eggs into toast cups. Bake at 375 degrees for 10 to 15 minutes, until golden. Sprinkle with remaining cheese; return to oven until cheese melts, about 2 minutes. Makes 5 servings.

Salt & pepper is a must for eggs and potatoes at breakfast. It's the perfect time to use Grandma's vintage rooster-shaped shakers for a sweet rise & shine greeting!

BREAKFAST IS SERVED... TIME TO GET UP!

Brown Sugar-Glazed Bacon

Bet you thought bacon couldn't get any better!

1 lb. bacon
1/3 c. brown sugar, packed

1 t. all-purpose flour
1/2 c. pecans, finely chopped

Cut bacon slices in half, if desired. Set a wire rack on a baking sheet. Arrange bacon slices on rack, close together but not overlapping. Combine brown sugar, flour and pecans in a small bowl; sprinkle evenly over bacon. Bake at 350 degrees for about 30 minutes, until bacon is crisp and glazed. Drain bacon on paper towels before serving. Serves 8.

Treat yourself to a buttery slice of cinnamon toast. Spread softened butter generously on one side of toasted white bread and sprinkle with cinnamon-sugar. Broil for one to 2 minutes, until bubbly and golden.

It's the Berries! French Toast

For making French toast, day-old bread holds its shape better than very fresh bread, so go ahead and use up that loaf.

3 eggs, beaten
3/4 c. half-and-half
1 T. strawberry jam
8 thick slices French bread

2 to 3 T. butter
Garnish: sliced strawberries,
powdered sugar

In a shallow bowl, whisk together eggs, half-and-half and jam. Melt butter in a large skillet over medium heat. Dip bread slices into egg mixture on both sides; cook until golden on both sides. Serve warm toast slices topped with a large dollop of Strawberry Butter, strawberries and a dusting of powdered sugar. Serves 4.

Strawberry Butter:

1/3 c. strawberry jam

1/4 c. butter, softened

Beat jam and butter with an electric mixer on low speed until well blended. Serve at room temperature.

For another berry delicious pancake & waffle topping, add 1/2 cup fresh blueberries, 1/2 cup softened butter and one tablespoon honey to a blender. Process until smooth.

BREAKFAST IS SERVED...
TIME TO GET UP!

Cinnamon-Sugar Mini Doughnuts

A basketful of warm sugary doughnuts to enjoy with your coffee, ready in just a few minutes? It's almost like magic!

7-1/2 oz. tube refrigerated
    biscuits
1/2 t. cinnamon

1/2 c. sugar
2 T. oil

Separate biscuits; cut each biscuit into 4 pieces. Combine cinnamon and sugar in a shallow bowl; set aside. Heat oil in a large skillet over medium-high heat. Add biscuits to hot oil, several at a time. Cook until golden on both sides; drain on paper towels and roll in cinnamon-sugar. Serve warm. Makes about 2-1/2 dozen.

Kitchen Cafe Mocha

Add even more flavor to your cup of coffee. Simply wet the paper filter before brewing as usual.

6 c. hot brewed coffee
3/4 c. half-and-half
6 T. chocolate syrup

2 T. plus 1 t. sugar, or to taste
Garnish: whipped cream,
    chocolate syrup

In a large saucepan, combine all ingredients except garnish. Cook and stir over medium heat until sugar is dissolved and mixture is heated through. Pour into mugs; top with a dollop of whipped cream and a drizzle of chocolate syrup. Makes 6 servings.

Perk up morning place settings in a wink...fill pint-size jelly jars with cheery blooms.

Delicious Doughnuts

This recipe makes enough for an army of hungry doughnut fans...or just enough for Garfield, preferably with a pot of coffee. Remember to mix up the dough ahead of time so it can rise.

2 c. buttermilk
3 eggs, beaten
1/3 c. shortening
7 c. all-purpose flour, divided
2 c. sugar
1 t. baking soda
2 t. salt
1 t. nutmeg

1/2 t. cinnamon
canola or peanut oil for deep
  frying
Garnish: powdered sugar,
  cinnamon-sugar or
  Powdered Sugar Glaze
  (see page 211)

Blend together buttermilk, eggs and shortening in a large bowl; set aside. In a separate bowl, mix together 2 cups flour, sugar, baking soda, salt and spices. Add flour mixture to buttermilk mixture; stir well. Mix in remaining flour. Cover and refrigerate for 8 hours to overnight. Roll out dough on a lightly floured surface, 1/3-inch thick. Cut out doughnuts with a 3" doughnut cutter. Add 3 inches of oil to a heavy stockpot. Heat oil to 365 degrees over medium-high heat. Add doughnuts and holes, a few at a time; cook until golden on both sides, about 2 minutes. Drain on paper towels. Sprinkle with powdered sugar or cinnamon-sugar, or drizzle with Powdered Sugar Glaze. Makes 4 to 5 dozen.

Don't have a deep-frying thermometer? Here's how to tell when the oil is hot enough. Drop a bread cube into the hot oil... if it turns golden in 60 seconds, the oil is ready.

Pumpkin Flapjacks

Too yummy not to enjoy year 'round!

1 c. all-purpose flour
2 T. dark brown sugar, packed
2 t. baking powder
1 t. pumpkin pie spice
1 c. canned pumpkin

1 c. milk
2 eggs, separated
1/3 c. oil
Garnish: butter, maple syrup

In a large bowl, combine flour, brown sugar, baking powder and spice; stir well and set aside. In a separate bowl, blend together pumpkin, milk and egg yolks. Add pumpkin mixture to flour mixture; stir until smooth. In a deep bowl, beat egg whites with an electric mixer on high speed until stiff peaks form. Gently fold egg whites into pumpkin mixture. Ladle batter by 1/3 cupfuls onto a hot greased griddle over medium heat. Cook pancakes until bubbly on top and edges are slightly dry; turn and cook on other side. Serve warm with butter and syrup. Makes about one dozen.

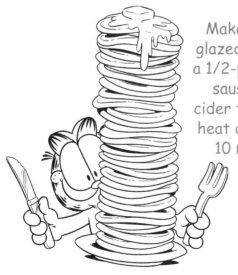

Make some scrumptious cider-glazed sausages. Brown and drain a 1/2-pound package of breakfast sausages. Add a cup of apple cider to the skillet, then turn the heat down to low and simmer for 10 minutes. It's that simple!

Light & Fluffy Pancakes

Who knew teeny could taste so good? Garfield finds these petite treats irresistible. This recipe will make about 30 small pancakes if you add batter by the tablespoonful.

1 c. all-purpose flour
2 T. sugar
2 t. baking powder
1/2 t. salt

1 egg, beaten
1 c. milk
2 T. oil
Garnish: butter

In a bowl, stir together flour, sugar, baking powder and salt. Add egg, milk and oil; stir until batter is blended but still slightly lumpy. Pour batter by 1/4 cupfuls onto a hot, lightly greased griddle. Cook on both sides until golden, turning when surface is bubbly and edges are slightly dry. Serve pancakes topped with butter and Luscious Blueberry Syrup. Makes 6 to 8 servings.

Luscious Blueberry Syrup:

1/2 c. sugar
1 T. cornstarch

1/3 c. water
2 c. fresh or frozen blueberries

Combine sugar and cornstarch in a saucepan over medium heat. Gradually stir in water. Add berries; bring to a boil. Boil, stirring constantly, for one minute, or until thickened. Serve warm.

Garfield on a slice of toast? Why not? "Paint" a face on toast just for fun! Combine one tablespoon of milk and 3 drops of food coloring, "paint" on bread, then pop in the toaster.

Kitchen Cupboard Waffles

Delicious golden waffles from scratch, no mix needed!

2 c. all-purpose flour
2 T. sugar
4 t. baking powder
1 t. salt

2 eggs, separated
1-1/2 c. milk
6 T. butter, melted and cooled
  slightly

Mix together flour, sugar, baking powder and salt in a large bowl. In a separate small bowl, whisk together egg yolks and milk. Stir yolk mixture into flour mixture, followed by butter. In a separate bowl, beat egg whites with an electric mixer on high speed until stiff. Fold egg whites into batter with a spoon. Pour batter, 1/2 cup at a time, onto a hot greased waffle iron. Bake according to manufacturer's instructions. Serve waffles topped with Buttery Maple Syrup. Serves 6.

Buttery Maple Syrup:

1/2 c. maple syrup
1/2 c. water

1/4 c. butter, sliced
Optional: cinnamon to taste

Combine all ingredients in a saucepan over low heat. Cook and stir until butter is melted. Serve warm.

Extra waffles and pancakes can be frozen in plastic freezer bags for up to a month. Reheat them in a toaster for a hearty, quick weekday breakfast.

Dieting

Mornings

Get cooking! But first...

-  Read the recipe through to avoid any surprises

- Make sure you have all the ingredients you need

- Turn on the oven if you are going to be baking

- Wash your hands, put on an apron and...

Have fun cooking!

Orange Streusel Coffee Cake

The best eye-opener ever...a citrusy slice of warm coffee cake with a mug of steaming-hot coffee!

2-1/4 c. all-purpose flour, divided
1 c. sugar, divided
2 t. baking powder
1 t. salt
1 T. orange zest

1 egg, beaten
1/2 c. milk
1/2 c. orange juice
1/2 c. oil
2 T. butter

In a large bowl, combine 2 cups flour, 1/2 cup sugar, baking powder and salt; mix well. Stir in orange zest. Make a well in the center of flour mixture and set aside. In a separate bowl, blend together egg, milk, orange juice and oil. Add egg mixture to well in flour mixture. Stir until moistened; batter will be lumpy. Pour batter into a greased 9" round cake pan. In another bowl, mix together butter, remaining flour and remaining sugar with a fork until crumbly; sprinkle evenly over batter. Bake at 375 degrees for 35 minutes, or until center tests clean with a toothpick. Cut into wedges. Makes 8 servings.

Grated citrus zest adds so much flavor to all kinds of recipes...and it's practically free! Whenever you use an orange or lemon, grate the peel first. Keep it frozen in an airtight container for up to two months.

Almond Coffee Cake

*Sprinkle some toasted sliced almonds over the batter
for extra crunchiness and almond flavor.*

1/4 c. shortening
1-1/3 c. sugar, divided
2 eggs, beaten
1-1/2 t. almond extract
2 t. baking powder

1/2 c. milk
1-1/2 c. all-purpose flour
1 T. cinnamon
Garnish: butter

Combine shortening and one cup sugar in a bowl; blend well. Stir in
eggs, extract and baking powder. Add milk and flour, a little at a time;
stir until smooth. Spread batter in a well-greased 11"x8" baking pan. In
a small bowl, mix cinnamon and remaining sugar. Sprinkle mixture
over batter. Bake at 350 degrees for 30 minutes, or until center tests
clean with a toothpick. Cut into squares. Serve warm, topped with
butter. Makes 8 to 10 servings.

Keep a tin of pumpkin pie spice on hand to jazz up pancakes,
muffins and coffee cakes. A quick shake adds cinnamon,
nutmeg and allspice all at once.

Upside-Down Apple Muffins

*Keep a box of colorful paper muffin cup liners in
the cupboard...speed up breakfast and turn it into a party too!*

1-1/2 c. all-purpose flour
1/2 c. sugar
2 t. baking powder
1/2 t. salt
1/2 t. cinnamon
1/2 t. nutmeg
1/4 c. plus 3 T. butter, divided

1/2 c. buttermilk
1 egg, beaten
1 Granny Smith apple, peeled,
  cored and grated
1/3 c. brown sugar, packed
1/2 c. chopped pecans

In a large bowl, combine flour, sugar, baking powder, salt and spices;
mix well. With a pastry cutter or 2 knives, cut in 1/4 cup butter until
mixture is crumbly. In a separate bowl, whisk together buttermilk and
egg. Add buttermilk mixture to flour mixture alternately with apple; stir
until moistened. Melt remaining butter; place in a cup and stir in brown
sugar. Divide brown sugar mixture evenly among 12 paper-lined or
greased muffin cups; top with pecans. Spoon batter evenly into muffin
cups. Bake at 375 degrees for about 20 minutes, until golden and
centers test clean with a toothpick. Turn muffins out of pan while still
warm; serve pecan-side up. Makes one dozen.

A baker's secret! Grease muffin cups on the bottoms
and just halfway up the sides...the muffins will
bake up nicely puffed on top.

Oatmeal-Blueberry Muffins

If it's wintertime and fresh blueberries are hard to find, just plump some dried berries in hot water. Drain and bake as usual.

1 egg
1 c. buttermilk
1/2 c. brown sugar, packed
1/3 c. butter, melted and cooled
   slightly
1 c. all-purpose flour

1 c. quick-cooking oats,
   uncooked
1 t. baking powder
1/2 t. baking soda
1 t. salt
1 c. blueberries

Combine egg, buttermilk, brown sugar and butter in a bowl; beat well. Add flour, oats, baking powder, baking soda and salt; stir just until moistened. Fold in blueberries. Spoon batter into 12 paper-lined or greased muffin cups, filling 2/3 full. Bake at 400 degrees for 20 minutes, or until golden. Makes one dozen.

If a muffin recipe doesn't fill all the cups in your muffin tin, add some water to the empty cups. This allows the muffins to bake more evenly.

Zazzy Zucchini Bread

This recipe makes two loaves of yummy bread...
one to enjoy today and one to freeze for later.

3 eggs, beaten
1 c. oil
2 c. sugar
2 c. zucchini, peeled and grated
1 T. vanilla extract
3 c. all-purpose flour

1/2 t. baking powder
1 t. baking soda
1 t. salt
2 t. cinnamon
Optional: 1/2 c. chopped walnuts

Mix together eggs, oil, sugar and zucchini in a bowl; stir in vanilla.
In a separate large bowl, combine remaining ingredients except
walnuts. Add flour mixture to zucchini mixture and stir well; mix in
walnuts, if using. Divide batter evenly between 2 lightly greased
8"x4" loaf pans. Bake at 325 degrees for one hour. Cool loaves slightly
in pans; turn out and cool on a wire rack. To freeze, cool completely,
then wrap in aluminum foil and plastic freezer wrap. Makes 2 loaves.

Applesauce can be used as a fat-free substitute for oil when
baking muffins and baking powder breads. Just substitute
the same amount of applesauce as the recipe calls for oil.

Monkey Bread

Grab a pair of kitchen scissors to cut up the biscuits in a hurry.

2 12-oz. tubes refrigerated
   biscuits
1/2 c. butter

1 c. brown sugar, packed
3 T. cinnamon, divided
1/2 c. sugar

Separate biscuits; cut each biscuit into 4 pieces and set aside. In a small saucepan over low heat, melt butter, brown sugar and one tablespoon cinnamon. Cook and stir until bubbly; remove from heat. In a small bowl, mix together sugar and remaining cinnamon. Roll biscuit pieces in cinnamon-sugar; arrange in a greased Bundt® pan. Spoon butter mixture over top. Bake at 325 degrees for 30 minutes, or until golden. Let cool in pan for several minutes; place a serving plate over top of pan; carefully turn over and turn bread out of pan. Serve warm. Makes 10 to 12 servings.

Check out a nearby farmers' market for fresh fruits & vegetables, homemade baked goods, jams & jellies... everything you need for a farm-style breakfast!

Cream Cheese Danish

Mmm...homemade Danish! Make them a teensy bit healthier by using creamy Neufchâtel cheese with 1/3 less fat.

2 8-oz. tubes refrigerated
   crescent rolls, divided
8-oz. pkg. cream cheese,
   softened
3-oz. pkg. cream cheese,
   softened

1 c. sugar
1/4 c. butter, melted
1 c. powdered sugar
1/2 t. vanilla extract
3 T. milk

Unroll one tube of crescent rolls without separating rolls. Place in the bottom of an ungreased 13"x9" baking pan. In a bowl, blend together both packages of cream cheese and sugar; gently spread over rolls. Top with remaining tube of rolls; brush with butter. Bake at 350 degrees for 25 to 30 minutes, or until golden. In a small bowl, stir together powdered sugar, vanilla and milk to a glaze consistency; drizzle over top. Cut into squares; serve warm. Makes 12 to 14 servings.

A big square of red-checked homespun fabric makes a cozy liner for a basket of warm muffins or rolls. You don't even need to hem the edges...just pull away the threads to create a fringe.

BREAKFAST IS SERVED...
TIME TO GET UP!

Real Deal Cinnamon Rolls

Yes, you can make bakery-style cinnamon rolls! To test the water's temperature, sprinkle the heated water on your forearm. If it doesn't feel either hot or cold, the temperature is just right.

3/4 c. warm water
2 envs. active dry yeast
1/2 c. sugar
1 t. salt
2 eggs, beaten

1/2 c. shortening
1/2 c. plus 2 T. butter, softened
   and divided
4 c. all-purpose flour
cinnamon-sugar to taste

Heat water until very warm, about 110 to 115 degrees; place in a large bowl. Stir in yeast, sugar, salt, eggs, shortening and 1/2 cup butter; add flour and mix well. Knead dough on a lightly floured surface for about 5 minutes. Place dough in a lightly greased bowl. Cover with a tea towel. Place bowl in a warm place and let rise until double in bulk, about 45 minutes. Roll out dough on a floured surface into a large rectangle, 1/4-inch thick. Spread with remaining butter; sprinkle generously with cinnamon-sugar. Roll up dough jelly-roll style; cut into slices one-inch thick. Arrange slices on a greased baking sheet. Bake at 350 degrees for 15 to 20 minutes, until golden. Makes 12 to 14 servings.

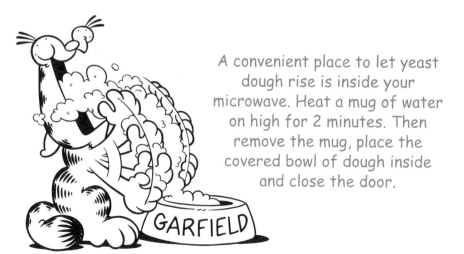

A convenient place to let yeast dough rise is inside your microwave. Heat a mug of water on high for 2 minutes. Then remove the mug, place the covered bowl of dough inside and close the door.

Lazy Cat Pancake

This pancake bakes in the oven...you don't even need to lift
a pancake turner! (No effort required...Garfield likes that.)

2 T. butter, melted
2 eggs, beaten
3-1/4 c. milk
1-2/3 c. all-purpose flour

1 t. salt
Garnish: raspberry jam,
   whipped cream

Spread butter in the bottom of a 13"x9" baking pan; set aside. Whisk
together eggs and milk in a large bowl. Add flour and salt; stir until
smooth. Pour batter into pan; do not stir. Bake at 425 degrees for
40 minutes, or until golden and top of pancake puffs up. Pancake will
fall when removed from oven. Let cool for 5 minutes. Cut into squares;
garnish with jam and whipped cream. Makes 3 to 4 servings.

Cook up some homemade applesauce to spoon over a
Lazy Cat Pancake while you're waiting for it to bake. Peel,
core and chop four tart apples. Place them in a saucepan
with 1/4 cup brown sugar, 1/4 cup water and 1/2 teaspoon
cinnamon. Cook over medium-low heat for 8 to 10 minutes,
until soft. Mash with a potato masher and serve warm.

BREAKFAST IS SERVED...
TIME TO GET UP!

Nuts & Honey Granola

Enjoy this crunchy granola topped with milk in a bowl, or carry it along in a small zipping bag to munch on anytime.

2 c. long-cooking oats,
   uncooked
1/2 c. sweetened flaked coconut
1/2 c. slivered almonds

1/2 c. sunflower kernels
1/2 c. honey
1/2 c. oil
1/4 c. dried cranberries

Combine oats, coconut, almonds and sunflower kernels in a bowl; toss to mix and set aside. In a separate bowl, stir together honey and oil. Drizzle honey mixture over oat mixture and stir well. Spread mixture onto a greased baking sheet. Bake at 300 degrees for 20 to 30 minutes, stirring once or twice, until toasty and golden. Remove from oven; cool completely and place in a large bowl. Add cranberries and toss to mix. Store in an airtight container. Makes about 4-1/2 cups.

A super-easy fresh breakfast side dish...fruit kabobs!
Just slide strawberries, melon cubes, pineapple
chunks, grapes, orange wedges and strawberries
onto wooden skewers.

Grab & Go Breakfast Cookies

You know Garfield would never miss his breakfast...why should you?
Take along one or two of these satisfying cookies.

1/2 c. butter, softened
1/2 c. sugar
1 egg
2 T. frozen orange juice
    concentrate, thawed

1 T. orange zest
1-1/4 c. all-purpose flour
1 t. baking powder
1/2 c. wheat & barley cereal
    nuggets

In a large bowl, blend together butter and sugar until light and fluffy. Beat in egg, orange juice and orange zest; set aside. In a small bowl, combine flour and baking powder; stir into butter mixture until mixed well. Stir in cereal. Drop by teaspoonfuls, 2 inches apart, on ungreased baking sheets. Bake at 350 degrees for 10 to 12 minutes, until edges are golden. Cool cookies on a wire rack. Makes 1-1/2 dozen.

Grab half a whole-grain bagel for a healthy breakfast. Toast it for extra flavor, then top with reduced-fat cream cheese and sliced strawberries.

BREAKFAST IS SERVED... TIME TO GET UP!

Breakfast Banana Split

Who says breakfast has to be serious? Treat your mouth to some fun!

1 banana
1/2 c. favorite crunchy cereal, divided
1/2 c. favorite fruit-flavored yogurt

1/4 c. strawberries, sliced, or blueberries
1/4 c. pineapple cubes
Garnish: maraschino cherry

Cut banana lengthwise down the middle. Place banana in a banana split dish or cereal bowl. Sprinkle with half of the cereal. Spoon yogurt over the banana and cereal. Sprinkle with remaining cereal; top with berries, pineapple and a cherry. Serve immediately. Makes one serving.

Frosty Orange Juice

Tastes like an orange & cream freezer pop!

6-oz. can frozen orange juice concentrate, partially thawed
1 c. milk
1 c. water

1 t. vanilla extract
1/3 c. sugar, or to taste
12 ice cubes

Combine all ingredients in a blender. Process until frothy. Pour into glasses and serve immediately. Makes 4 servings.

Make juice glasses sparkle!
Dip the rims in water and
roll in coarse sugar before
filling with juice.

Sticky Bun Toast Topper

Yum...tastes like a pecan sticky roll and it's ready in a jiffy!

2 T. brown sugar, packed
1 T. butter
1 T. light corn syrup
1/4 t. cinnamon

4 slices multi-grain or white
   bread, toasted
1/4 c. chopped pecans, toasted

Combine brown sugar, butter, corn syrup and cinnamon in a microwave-safe small bowl. Microwave on high setting for one minute. Stir; spread evenly over toast slices. Sprinkle with pecans. Makes 4 servings.

Dreamy Hot Chocolate

The perfect warmer-upper for a chilly morning.

14-oz. can regular or low-fat
   sweetened condensed milk
1/3 c. baking cocoa
2 t. vanilla extract

6 c. boiling water, divided
Optional: whipped cream,
   cinnamon

In a large saucepan over low heat, combine condensed milk and cocoa. Cook and stir until smooth and warm, 3 to 4 minutes. Add vanilla and one cup boiling water; mix well. Stir in remaining water. Serve in mugs, topped with whipped cream and cinnamon, if desired. Makes 6 to 8 servings.

Pick up a bunch of sunny daisies at the grocery store to tuck into a vintage milk bottle...what could be sweeter on the breakfast table?

First Lunch, Then a Catnap

The four basic food groups:
meat, vegetable, dairy and *catsup*

FIRST LUNCH, THEN A CATNAP

Delicious Patty Melts

*Much tastier than the patty melts down at Irma's Diner
(the greasy spoon frequented by Jon and Garfield). But don't tell
irritable Irma...she might sling some hash...literally!*

2 to 3 T. butter, softened and
    divided
1 onion, thinly sliced
1 lb. ground beef, formed into
    4 thin patties

seasoned salt and pepper
    to taste
8 slices rye bread
8 slices Swiss cheese

Melt one tablespoon butter in a skillet over medium heat; add onion.
Cook for 10 to 15 minutes, until onion is golden and caramelized.
Meanwhile, season beef patties with salt and pepper. On a griddle
over medium heat, brown patties for about 6 minutes on each side,
until no longer pink in center. Wipe griddle clean with a paper towel.
Spread remaining butter on one side of each bread slice; place 4 slices
butter-side down on hot griddle. Top each bread slice with a cheese
slice, a beef patty, 1/4 of onion, another cheese slice and another
bread slice, butter-side up. Cook sandwiches over medium-low heat
until golden on both sides and cheese is melted, about 5 minutes.
Makes 4 servings.

Juicy burgers start with ground beef chuck. A little fat
in the beef adds flavor...there's no need to pay more
for extra-lean ground sirloin!

Devilishly Good Burgers

You won't believe your taste buds! All-day marinating makes these burgers delicious, so be sure to mix 'em up ahead of time.

1 lb. ground beef	1 t. red steak sauce
2 T. catsup	1 t. seasoned salt
1 T. onion, chopped	1/2 t. pepper
2 t. mustard	4 hamburger buns, split

In a large bowl, combine all ingredients except buns. Mix well; form into 4 burgers. Cover and refrigerate for about 8 hours, to allow flavors to blend. Cook burgers to desired doneness by frying in a skillet, or grilling on a countertop grill or outdoor grill. Serve burgers on buns. Makes 4 servings.

Happy Burgers

Mmm...blue cheese and tomatoes. Happiness is a juicy burger!

1 lb. lean ground beef	1/2 t. salt
2/3 c. crumbled blue cheese	1/4 t. pepper
1/2 c. soft bread crumbs	4 to 6 cherry tomatoes, halved
1 egg, beaten	4 hamburger buns, split

In a large bowl, combine all ingredients except buns. Mix well; form into 4 burgers. Grill over medium-high heat to desired doneness, turning to cook on both sides. Serve burgers on buns. Makes 4 servings.

Slip your hands inside two plastic bags when shaping ground beef into burgers...no more messy hands! Just toss away the bags when you're finished.

FIRST LUNCH, THEN A CATNAP

Garlic Oven Fries

It's really easy to make French fries from scratch...give it a try!

4 baking potatoes
1/4 c. olive oil
2 t. salt

1 t. pepper
1-1/2 T. garlic, minced
Garnish: catsup

Peel potatoes, if desired. Cut potatoes lengthwise into 1/2-inch wide sticks. Place potatoes in a bowl and toss with oil, salt, pepper and garlic. Arrange potatoes in a single layer on an ungreased baking sheet. Bake at 400 degrees until potatoes are golden on the bottom, 20 to 30 minutes. Turn potatoes over. Continue baking another 10 to 15 minutes, until golden on both sides. Serve with catsup. Makes 4 servings.

Pick up a stack of diner-style plastic burger baskets.
Lined with checked paper napkins, they're lots of fun for
serving burgers, hot dogs and fries. Don't forget to
add a pickle spear!

Stuffed Pepper Soup

*This recipe makes enough soup for the whole gang! Freeze any
leftovers for a quick cup of homemade soup another day.*

1-1/2 lbs. ground beef
1 onion, chopped
1 T. butter
2-1/2 c. beef broth
2 10-3/4 oz. cans tomato soup
15-oz. can diced tomatoes

2 stalks celery, chopped
2 green peppers, chopped
2 cloves garlic, minced
1/8 t. sugar
salt and pepper to taste
1 c. cooked rice

In a soup pot over medium heat, brown beef and onion in butter;
drain. Add remaining ingredients except rice; mix well. Reduce heat to
low; cover and simmer for 45 minutes, stirring occasionally. Stir in
rice; simmer another 15 minutes. Makes 10 to 12 servings.

Super-easy homestyle tomato soup for two...just right
for sharing on a rainy day! Combine a can of tomato soup
with a can of diced tomatoes and simmer until hot.
Add a little Italian seasoning plus a bit of cream or
milk, if you like it creamy.

Deluxe Grilled Cheese

Don't settle for a boring grilled cheese sandwich! Try lots of other kinds of cheese too...chipotle Cheddar, anybody?

8 slices country-style bread
1 clove garlic, halved
4 t. Dijon mustard
8 slices Gouda cheese

2 T. butter, melted
1/8 t. cayenne pepper
1/8 t. pepper

Rub one side of each bread slice with the cut side of the garlic. Turn 4 bread slices garlic-side down; top each slice with one teaspoon mustard, 2 slices cheese and another bread slice, garlic-side up. Combine butter and peppers in a small bowl; brush over both sides of sandwiches. Toast sandwiches in an oven-proof skillet over medium-high heat for about 2 minutes on each side, until golden. Place skillet in oven and bake at 400 degrees for about 5 minutes, until cheese is melted. Slice sandwiches in half diagonally. Serves 4.

Love grilled cheese, but you're counting calories? Spritz the bread with butter-flavored non-stick vegetable spray instead of spreading with butter. Use low-fat (not fat-free) cheese, and cook the sandwich over low heat to allow the cheese to melt without becoming tough.

5-Alarm Chili

A quick trick if you like your chili extra-thick...stir in a can of refried beans!

1 lb. ground beef
1 onion, diced
1 clove garlic, minced
2 to 3 t. chili powder
16-oz. jar medium or hot salsa
15-oz. can tomato sauce
14-oz. can stewed tomatoes

14-oz. can kidney beans,
    drained and rinsed
14-oz. can pinto beans, drained
    and rinsed
3 T. Worcestershire sauce
Garnish: saltine crackers,
    shredded Cheddar cheese

Brown beef in a Dutch oven over medium heat. Add onion, garlic and chili powder. Cook, stirring often, until onion is translucent and chili powder is fragrant; drain. Stir in remaining ingredients except garnish; bring to a boil. Reduce heat to low; simmer for 20 to 30 minutes, until heated through. Garnish as desired. Serves 6.

Cheesy Chili Dogs

Don't have a slow cooker? Combine the hot dogs and the chili mixture in a saucepan and simmer over low heat for 45 minutes.

8 to 10 hot dogs
2 15-oz. cans chili,
    or 4 c. homemade chili
10-3/4 oz. can Cheddar cheese
    soup
4-oz. can chopped green chiles

8 to 10 hot dog buns, split
Garnish: chopped onion,
    shredded Cheddar cheese,
    crushed chili-cheese
    corn chips

Place hot dogs in a slow cooker. Mix chili, soup and chiles in a bowl; spoon over hot dogs. Cover and cook on low setting for 3 to 3-1/2 hours. Serve hot dogs in buns; top with chili mixture from slow cooker. Garnish as desired. Makes 8 to 10 servings.

Lazy-Does-It Beefy Lasagna Soup

Stir up this spoonable lasagna in your slow cooker, then take a long nap...it doesn't get much lazier than that!

1 lb. ground beef, browned
   and drained
15-oz. can Italian-style stewed
   tomatoes
6 c. water

6.4-oz. pkg. lasagna dinner
   mix, divided
Garnish: grated Parmesan
   cheese

In a slow cooker, combine beef, undrained tomatoes, water and sauce packet from dinner mix; stir well. Cover and cook on low setting for 4 to 6 hours. Stir in uncooked lasagna noodles from dinner mix. Cover and cook an additional 20 minutes, until noodles are tender. Garnish individual bowls with Parmesan cheese. Makes 6 servings.

Parmesan Bread Sticks

Enjoy these yummy golden bread sticks with hot soup, spaghetti or even as a snack while you're waiting for the pizza to bake.

1/3 c. butter, melted
1 t. dried rosemary
1 clove garlic, minced
2-1/4 c. all-purpose flour

2 T. grated Parmesan cheese
1 T. sugar
3-1/2 t. baking powder
1 c. milk

Spread butter in a 13"x9" baking pan, tilting to coat pan. Sprinkle with rosemary and garlic; set aside. In a bowl, combine flour, cheese, sugar and baking powder; stir in milk until a soft dough forms. Turn dough onto a floured surface; knead until smooth. Roll out into a 12-inch by 6-inch rectangle; cut into strips one-inch wide. Twist each strip 6 times; place in pan. Bake at 400 degrees for 20 to 25 minutes, until golden. Serve warm. Makes one dozen.

Super Stacked Sandwich

This party-size sandwich has something for everyone in it!

12-inch round pumpernickel loaf
1/2 c. mayonnaise
1/4 c. coarse-grain mustard
1/2 lb. thinly sliced deli honey
   ham
1/2 lb. thinly sliced deli
   peppered turkey

1/2 lb. thinly sliced deli chicken
   breast
1 to 2 tomatoes, thinly sliced
1 red onion, thinly sliced
8 slices Cheddar cheese
2 c. shredded lettuce

Cut loaf in half horizontally. In a small bowl, blend mayonnaise and mustard; spread on cut sides of loaf. Layer remaining ingredients on bottom half of loaf; add top half of loaf. Cut into wedges and serve immediately, or wrap well with plastic wrap and refrigerate up to 2 hours. Serves 8 to 12.

Be ready anytime for an instant picnic! Tuck a basket filled with picnic supplies in the car along with a blanket to sit on. One stop at a deli or a roadside stand for food, and it's picnic time.

Italian Meatball Subs

Wanna make your own meatballs? Use the recipe on page 77, but simmer the meatballs right in the pizza sauce until they're done.

1 onion, sliced
1/2 c. green pepper, chopped
2 T. water
2 15-oz. cans pizza sauce
24 meatballs, thawed if frozen

4 Italian hard rolls, partially
   sliced and hollowed out
1/2 to 3/4 c. shredded provolone
   cheese

In a large saucepan over medium heat, combine onion, pepper and water. Cover and cook just until vegetables are tender, about 5 minutes; drain. Stir in pizza sauce and meatballs. Simmer until hot and bubbly, 5 to 10 minutes. Fill each roll with 6 meatballs; top with some of the sauce. Sprinkle with cheese. Close rolls and place in an ungreased 13"x9" baking pan. Bake at 400 degrees for 10 to 15 minutes, until rolls are toasty and cheese is melted. Serve with remaining sauce for dipping. Makes 4 servings.

Stem and seed a green pepper in a flash...hold the pepper upright on a cutting board. Use a sharp knife to slice each of the sides from the pepper. You'll then have four large seedless pieces ready for chopping!

Mom's Chicken Soup for a Cold

...or just to warm you up inside & out! Jon's mom sends this soup home from the farm in giant jars.

1 T. olive oil
1 c. celery, chopped
1/2 c. onion, chopped
2 T. garlic, minced
5 to 6 chicken thighs
2 c. baby carrots, chopped
3 cubes chicken bouillon

1 t. poultry seasoning
1 t. dried parsley
1 t. seasoned salt
pepper to taste
12-oz. pkg. fine egg noodles, uncooked

Heat oil in a large soup pot over medium heat. Add celery and onion; cook for 5 minutes. Stir in garlic and cook another 2 minutes; drain. Add chicken, carrots, bouillon, seasonings and enough water to cover. Bring to a boil over medium heat; reduce heat to low. Simmer, uncovered, for 45 minutes to one hour, or until chicken and vegetables are very tender. Remove chicken to a plate. Dice chicken when cooled, discarding skin and bones. Stir chicken and noodles into hot soup in pot. Simmer until noodles are tender, about 5 to 8 minutes. Add a little more seasoned salt, if desired. Makes 8 servings.

Homemade soup tastes even better if it's made a day ahead of time and refrigerated overnight. As a bonus, any fat will rise to the top, where it's easy to lift off and discard.

FIRST LUNCH, THEN A CATNAP

Grilled Peanut Butter & Jelly

Something different for lunch or even breakfast! Just for fun, toast these sandwiches on a waffle iron instead of a griddle.

8 slices whole-wheat or
    white bread
1/4 c. creamy peanut butter
1/4 c. grape jelly or
    strawberry jam

1 egg, beaten
1/4 c. milk
1 T. vanilla extract
1 t. cinnamon
1 to 2 T. butter

Spread 4 slices of bread with peanut butter and jelly or jam; top with remaining bread. Whisk together remaining ingredients except butter in a shallow bowl. Brush egg mixture over one side of sandwiches. Melt butter on a griddle over medium heat. Add sandwiches to griddle, egg-side down; brush remaining mixture over top. Cook, turning once, until golden on both sides; slice in half. Makes 4 servings.

Country Buttermilk Biscuits

Jon's mom shared her farmhouse secret to light-as-a-feather biscuits...stop stirring the batter as soon as it's moistened.

2-1/2 c. all-purpose flour
3 T. sugar
1-1/2 T. baking powder

1/4 t. salt
1/2 c. butter, softened
1 c. buttermilk

In a bowl, combine flour, sugar, baking powder and salt; mix well. Add butter and buttermilk; stir just until moistened. Spoon batter into 12 to 18 greased muffin cups. Bake at 350 degrees for 30 minutes, or until golden. Serve warm. Makes one to 1-1/2 dozen.

Make biscuit toppers for bowls of homemade chicken soup.
Flatten unbaked biscuits into 6-inch circles and bake
them as usual, until golden. Top each soup bowl
with a biscuit and dig in!

51

Bacon Burgers

Everyone loves these burgers...maybe you'd better
make a double batch. (Triple if Garfield is coming!)

2 to 3 slices bacon
2 T. onion, chopped
1/3 c. sliced mushrooms
1/2 lb. ground beef
1/2 lb. ground pork sausage

2 T. grated Parmesan cheese
1 T. steak sauce
1/4 t. garlic powder
1/4 t. pepper
4 sesame sandwich buns, split

In a skillet over medium heat, cook bacon until crisp. Set aside bacon;
reserve one tablespoon drippings in skillet. Add onion and mushrooms
to skillet; cook until tender. Crumble bacon and return to skillet;
remove from heat. In a large bowl, combine beef, sausage, cheese,
steak sauce and seasonings. Mix well; form into 8 thin patties. Spoon
onion mixture over 4 patties. Top with remaining patties; press edges
tightly to seal. Cook burgers to desired doneness on a grill or in a
skillet over medium heat. Serve burgers on buns. Makes 4 servings.

When burgers, hot dogs, tacos or baked potatoes are on
the menu, set up a topping bar with bowls of shredded
cheese, catsup or salsa, crispy bacon and other yummy
stuff. Everyone can just help themselves to
their favorite toppings!

Grilled Dogs & Kraut

Turn 'em into Reuben dogs...stir in some shredded Swiss cheese.

3 slices bacon
1/2 to 3/4 c. Thousand Island
   salad dressing

3/4 c. sauerkraut, drained
8 hot dogs
8 hot dog buns, split and toasted

In a skillet over medium heat, cook bacon until crisp; drain. Combine salad dressing, sauerkraut and bacon in a bowl; set aside. Grill hot dogs to desired doneness, or simmer in a saucepan of water until hot. Place hot dogs in buns; top with spoonfuls of bacon mixture. Makes 8 servings.

The easiest way ever to make crispy bacon! Place bacon slices on a broiler pan. Bake at 400 degrees for 12 to 15 minutes. Turn bacon over and bake for another 8 to 10 minutes. Toss on a few extra slices for your next BLT!

Hearty Sausage & Bean Soup

Substitute baby spinach or Swiss chard for the kale, if you like.

1/2 lb. Kielbasa sausage, sliced
1 onion, chopped
3 cloves garlic, minced
1 potato, peeled and cubed
1 lb. fresh kale, trimmed and
    chopped
2 14-1/2 oz. cans chicken broth

15-oz. can Great Northern
    beans, drained and rinsed
1 t. dried thyme
1 t. pepper
Garnish: shredded Parmesan
    cheese

In a stockpot over medium heat, combine sausage, onion, garlic, potato and kale. Cook for 5 minutes, stirring frequently, or until sausage browns and kale begins to wilt. Stir in remaining ingredients except cheese. Bring to a boil; reduce heat to medium-low. Simmer, partially covered, for 10 to 12 minutes, until potato is tender. Top individual soup bowls with cheese. Makes 6 to 8 servings.

Keep a container in the freezer for leftover bits of cooked meat and veggies. When the container gets full, toss everything in a big soup pot with some tomato juice, simmer it for 30 minutes or so and you'll have a tasty mixed-up soup that's never the same twice!

Mom's Farmhouse Cornbread

Wanna make corn muffins instead? Fill greased muffin cups 2/3 full and bake, checking for doneness after 15 minutes.

1 c. all-purpose flour
3/4 c. yellow cornmeal
2/3 c. sugar
3-1/2 t. baking powder
3/4 t. salt

1 c. milk
1 egg, beaten
1/4 c. oil
Garnish: butter

In a bowl, stir together flour, cornmeal, sugar, baking powder and salt. Make a well in the center and set aside. In a separate bowl, whisk together milk, egg and oil; pour into well in flour mixture. Beat thoroughly. Pour batter into a greased 8"x8" baking pan. Bake at 400 degrees for 22 to 25 minutes, until center is set and edges are golden. Cut into squares; serve warm with butter. Makes 10 to 12 servings.

Cornbread and hot soup are made for each other!
Shake up this cornbread recipe by stirring in some
shredded Cheddar cheese, crispy bacon, diced
green chiles or fresh corn kernels.

Kitchen Basics

Measure

Liquids – Use a glass measuring cup, fill to the marked line.

Solids – Use a plastic or metal measuring cup or spoon, fill to the top and level off with a table knife.

Slice & Dice

Chop – Cut into bite-size pieces, not too small.

Cube – Cut into cubes, 1/2 inch or more.

Dice – Cut into small cubes, 1/2 inch or less.

Mince – Cut into very small pieces.

Sauté

Cook and stir in oil in a skillet over medium heat.

Simmer

Bring to a boil, turn down the heat and cook slowly, without quite boiling.

Bake

Preheat the oven by turning it on 10 minutes before the pan goes in.

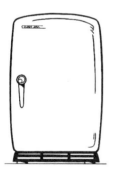

Chill

Place the dish in the fridge (not the freezer) until chilled through.

Time

Set a kitchen timer & check after the shortest time given.

Crispy Corn Dogs

Yummy...no more waiting for the carnival to come to town!
Pour the batter into a tall jar for easy dunking.

8 to 10 hot dogs
8 to 10 wooden skewers
   or chopsticks
1 c. yellow cornmeal
1 c. all-purpose flour
1/2 c. sugar

4 t. baking powder
2 t. salt
1 egg, beaten
1 c. milk
canola oil for deep frying
Garnish: mustard, catsup

Pat hot dogs dry with a paper towel. Insert sticks in hot dogs and set aside. In a bowl, stir together cornmeal, flour, sugar, baking powder and salt. Add egg and milk; beat until smooth. In a deep skillet over medium-high heat, heat several inches of oil to 365 degrees. Dip hot dogs in batter and add to oil, 2 to 3 at a time. Cook, turning hot dogs often, until golden on all sides. Place on paper towels to drain. Serve with mustard and catsup. Makes 8 to 10 servings.

For the crispest corn dogs, French fries and other
fried foods, drain them on a wire rack that's
been set over a paper towel-lined baking sheet.

Golden Onion Rings

*Try Japanese-style panko bread crumbs for an extra crispy crust...
they're found right next to regular dry bread crumbs.*

2-1/2 c. all-purpose flour
2 t. baking powder
2 t. salt
2 to 3 sweet onions, thickly
    sliced and separated
    into rings

2 eggs, beaten
2 c. milk
1-1/2 c. dry bread crumbs
olive oil for deep frying
salt and pepper to taste

In a shallow bowl, stir together flour, baking powder and salt. Coat
onion rings with flour mixture; set aside. Add eggs and milk to
remaining flour mixture; whisk well. Dip floured onion rings into egg
mixture; drain on a wire rack. Coat onion rings with bread crumbs. In a
large saucepan, heat several inches oil to 365 degrees. Fry onion rings,
a few at a time, for 2 to 3 minutes, until golden on all sides. Drain on
paper towels. Sprinkle with salt and pepper; serve warm. Serves 6.

Set aside a few uncooked slices of sweet onion...they're
delicious on your favorite burgers!

Cheesy Burgers

Tasting is believing! Load up these big burgers with tomato slices, pickle chips, onion slices, catsup and mustard...the works!

2/3 c. shredded provolone
   cheese
1/2 c. green pepper, diced
1/2 c. onion, diced
salt and pepper to taste

2 lbs. ground beef
4 to 6 sesame seed kaiser rolls,
   split
Optional: additional shredded
   provolone cheese

Toss together cheese, green pepper, onion, salt and pepper in a large bowl. Add beef; mix well and form into 4 to 6 burgers. Add burgers to a skillet over medium-high heat. Cook for 4 to 5 minutes on each side, to desired doneness. Serve burgers on rolls, topped with extra cheese, if desired. Serves 4 to 6.

Burger buns just taste better toasted...and they won't get soggy! Butter buns lightly and place them on a hot grill for 30 seconds to one minute on each side, until toasty.

FIRST LUNCH, THEN A CATNAP

Baked Chili Fries

Frozen steak fries can be fixed this way too. Just bake them at the temperature and time in the package directions.

1 t. chili powder
1 t. onion powder
1 t. garlic powder
1 t. seasoned salt
3 T. olive oil

3 baking potatoes, cut into
   wedges
Garnish: catsup, ranch salad
   dressing

Mix seasonings in a large plastic zipping bag. Add oil and squeeze to mix; add potato wedges. Seal bag tightly; shake vigorously to coat potatoes well. Arrange potatoes on an aluminum foil-lined baking sheet. Bake at 400 degrees for 15 minutes. Turn potatoes over and bake another 15 minutes, or until tender and golden. Serve with catsup and ranch salad dressing for dipping. Makes 4 to 6 servings.

For recipes like Spicy Baked Chili Fries that you make often, mix up several small bags of the seasoning blend. Label with the recipe's name and tuck in the cupboard...a terrific time-saver for future meals!

Tuna-Egg Salad Sandwiches

Tuck in some avocado slices for an even tastier sandwich.

4 eggs, hard-boiled, peeled
    and chopped
12-oz. can tuna, drained
2 T. red onion, minced
3 T. mayonnaise
2 T. honey mustard

salt and pepper to taste
8 slices whole-wheat or
    white bread
4 leaves lettuce
4 slices tomato
1 c. alfalfa sprouts

In a bowl, blend together eggs, tuna, onion, mayonnaise, mustard, salt and pepper. Spread mixture evenly over 4 bread slices. Top each slice with one lettuce leaf, one tomato slice and 1/4 cup alfalfa sprouts. Top sandwiches with remaining bread slices; slice in half. Makes 4 servings.

Hard-boiled eggs made easy! Cover eggs with an inch of water in a saucepan and place over medium-high heat. As soon as the water boils, cover the pan and remove from heat. Let stand for 18 to 20 minutes...cover with ice water, peel and they're done.

Horseradish Dill Pickles

These pickles aren't too hot...just full of flavor! They're super-easy to make too. Start a week ahead so that the pickles can absorb all the flavors.

16-oz. jar whole kosher
  dill pickles
1/4 c. prepared horseradish

1/3 c. white vinegar
2-1/2 T. water
3/4 c. sugar

Drain pickle juice from jar into a bowl; set aside. Remove pickles from jar. Trim ends and cut each pickle lengthwise into 4 spears; set aside in a separate bowl. Wash empty jar well. Spoon horseradish into jar; return pickles to jar and set aside. Combine vinegar, water and sugar in a saucepan over medium-high heat. Bring to a boil; stir until sugar dissolves and remove from heat. Pour vinegar mixture over pickles in jar; add enough of the reserved pickle juice to fill the jar. Close jar with lid; shake jar vigorously to mix well. Keep refrigerated for one week before serving, shaking jar once a day. Makes about 8 to 10 servings.

Next time you finish a jar of dill pickles, use the leftover juice to make some crunchy, tangy pickled veggies! Cut up fresh carrots, green peppers, celery and other favorite veggies, add them to the pickle juice and refrigerate for a few days.

Potato, Ham & Cheddar Soup

Sprinkle a little extra cheese on top of each bowl...scrumptious!

2 c. potatoes, peeled and diced
1/2 c. carrot, peeled and diced
1/2 c. celery, chopped
1/4 c. onion, chopped
2 c. water
1-1/2 t. salt
1/4 t. pepper

1 c. cooked ham, cubed
1/4 c. butter
1/4 c. all-purpose flour
2 c. milk
8-oz. pkg. shredded Cheddar
    cheese

Combine vegetables, water, salt and pepper in a large soup pot. Bring to a boil over medium heat. Reduce heat to low. Cover and simmer until vegetables are tender, about 15 minutes. Stir in ham; set aside. In a separate saucepan, melt butter; stir in flour until smooth. Gradually add milk; bring to a boil. Cook and stir for 2 minutes, until thickened. Add cheese; stir until melted. Stir cheese mixture into soup; heat through. Serves 8.

Soups and main dishes are delicious ways to make a second meal out of leftover ham. But if you don't have any, just go to the deli counter and buy 2 or 3 thick-cut slices of ham to use instead. Problem solved!

FIRST LUNCH, THEN A CATNAP

A-to-Z Vegetable Soup

So convenient...just keep all the ingredients in the kitchen cupboard, pantry or freezer, then stir up some homemade soup in 30 minutes!

1 onion, coarsely chopped
2 cloves garlic, minced
1 to 2 T. olive oil
1 to 2 T. Italian seasoning
3 14-1/2 oz. cans beef or
   vegetable broth

15-oz. can stewed tomatoes
16-oz. pkg. frozen mixed
   vegetables
1/2 c. alphabet pasta, uncooked
salt and pepper to taste
3 T. fresh parsley, minced

In a large soup pot over medium heat, cook onion and garlic in oil until onion is golden, about 8 minutes. Add seasoning to taste; cook and stir for one minute. Add broth and undrained tomatoes, breaking up tomatoes as you add them to the pot. Bring to a boil. Reduce heat to medium-low and simmer for 10 minutes. Stir in frozen vegetables and pasta. Cover and simmer until pasta is tender, about 10 to 12 minutes. Add salt and pepper; stir in parsley. Serves 6 to 8.

Banish rainy-day boredom! Set kids down with a box of alphabet pasta, a bottle of white craft glue and a stack of colored paper...they can spell out as many names and phrases as they like.

Indiana Chicken-Corn Chowder

If you prefer, use fresh corn and potatoes for this satisfying soup, straight out of the Hoosier heartland. You'll need about 4 cups of each veggie.

3 c. water
32-oz. pkg. frozen corn
32-oz. pkg. frozen diced
   potatoes
1/4 c. carrot, peeled and diced
2 T. celery, diced
1 T. dried, chopped onion
1 c. cooked chicken, diced

salt and pepper to taste
6 slices bacon, crisply cooked
   and crumbled
5-oz. can evaporated milk
1 c. half-and-half
Optional: 1/2 c. instant mashed
   potato flakes

In a large soup kettle over medium-high heat, combine water, vegetables, chicken, salt and pepper. Bring to a boil. Reduce heat to low; cover and simmer for 15 minutes, or until vegetables are tender. Add bacon, milk and half-and-half; heat through. If a thicker chowder is desired, stir in potato flakes to desired consistency. Makes 8 servings.

Eat-it-all bread bowls make hearty soup extra special. Cut the tops off round loaves of bread and hollow out, then rub with olive oil and garlic. Pop bread bowls in the oven at 400 degrees for 10 minutes, or until crusty and golden. Ladle in soup and enjoy!

Jim Davis's Spicy Deviled Eggs

Garfield's creator, Jim Davis, created this tasty recipe. Jim, a good egg...but a little cracked...thinks it's not a picnic without at least a platter of deviled eggs. Better yet, he says to bring enough for the ants, too!

6 eggs
1/8 c. mayonnaise or
    mayonnaise-style salad
    dressing
1/8 c. horseradish sauce

1 t. spicy mustard
1/2 t. vinegar
1 T. sweet pickle relish
salt and pepper to taste
Garnish: paprika

Place eggs in a saucepan; add water to cover. Bring to a boil over medium heat. Reduce heat to low; cover and simmer for 15 minutes. Remove saucepan from heat; drain and run cold water over eggs for several minutes. Peel eggs and cut in half; arrange egg white halves on a serving plate. Remove egg yolks to a bowl and mash with a fork. Add remaining ingredients except garnish; mix well. Spoon egg yolk mixture into a cookie press; fill egg whites with mixture. Garnish with a light dusting of paprika. Cover and refrigerate until serving time. Makes 12 servings.

Making some yummy deviled eggs for a party or picnic? Whip 'em up in no time by spooning the egg yolk filling into a plastic zipping bag. Snip off a corner and pipe the filling into the egg white halves...easy squeezy!

Hawaiian Pizza Sub

Say "aloha" to this scrumptious sandwich in fresh-baked bread!

11-oz. tube refrigerated crusty
  French loaf
2 T. oil
1 t. Italian seasoning
1/4 t. garlic powder

8-oz. can pizza sauce, divided
1/3 lb. sliced deli ham
8-oz. can crushed pineapple,
  drained
1 c. shredded mozzarella cheese

Place loaf seam-side down on a greased baking sheet. Cut slashes on top, about 1/2 inch deep. Bake at 350 degrees for 25 to 30 minutes, until golden; remove from oven. Combine oil, Italian seasoning and garlic powder in a small bowl; brush over hot loaf. Let loaf cool for 10 minutes; slice in half horizontally. Hollow out bottom half of loaf, leaving a 1/4-inch shell. Spread bottom half with 2 tablespoons of pizza sauce. Layer with ham, pineapple, cheese and top half of loaf. Bake at 350 degrees for an additional 6 to 8 minutes. Slice and serve with remaining pizza sauce. Serves 4 to 6.

Mix up some tropical coleslaw in a jiffy. Combine a package of shredded coleslaw mix and bottled coleslaw dressing to taste. Stir in a drained can of mandarin oranges or pineapple tidbits for a sweet twist. Wonderful with a Hawaiian Pizza Sub...a perfect partner for spicy barbecue or crispy fish too!

Picnic Sweet Pickles

Sure to be the most popular item on the relish tray!

16-oz. jar whole dill pickles	1 c. sugar
2 T. white vinegar	3 whole cloves
2 T. water	4-inch cinnamon stick

Drain pickles, discarding juice; place pickles in a bowl. Wash empty jar and set aside. Rinse pickles well. Trim off ends of pickles, slice pickles into chunks and return to jar; set aside. In a saucepan over medium heat, mix remaining ingredients. Simmer for 5 minutes, stirring until sugar dissolves; do not boil. Pour vinegar mixture over pickles in jar; place lid on jar. Let stand at room temperature for 24 hours. Chill in refrigerator; remove spices at serving time. Return to refrigerator after jar is opened. Makes about 8 to 10 servings.

Pack a frozen bottle of lemonade or iced tea with lunch in the morning to keep everything cool. When lunchtime rolls around, enjoy a fresh, crisp sandwich and a frosty beverage too!

Deluxe Greek Salad

Garfield's idea of a diet salad is one leaf of lettuce and a quart of mayo. He'd like this much better if he just gave it a try!

16-oz. pkg. mixed salad greens
1 cucumber, sliced
1 red onion, thinly sliced
1 to 2 roma tomatoes, chopped
3-1/4 oz. can sliced black olives, drained
8-oz. container crumbled feta cheese

1/4 c. olive oil
1/4 c. lemon juice
2 cloves garlic, crushed
1 t. sugar
dried oregano, dried thyme and pepper to taste
1 c. salad croutons

In a large salad bowl, combine salad greens, vegetables and cheese. Toss to mix and set aside. In a jar with a tight-fitting lid, combine remaining ingredients except croutons; shake well. Just before serving, pour dressing over salad. Toss to coat; top with croutons. Makes 6 to 8 servings.

Make your own crispy croutons for soups and salads...they're so much tastier than the boxed kind! Toss cubes of day-old bread with olive oil and sprinkle with Italian seasoning or other dried herbs. Toast on a baking sheet at 400 degrees for 5 to 10 minutes, until golden.

A few of Garfield's favorite snacks
There isn't much he *won't* snack on...
day or night!

SNACK ATTACK!

Garfield's Pizza Bites

Garfield finds these perfect for bite-size bingeing. Ready to gobble down in just minutes...what are you waiting for?

8-oz. tube refrigerated crescent rolls
1/3 c. pizza sauce
1/4 c. grated Parmesan cheese

16 slices pepperoni
1/3 c. shredded mozzarella cheese

Unroll rolls but do not separate; press perforations to seal. Spread pizza sauce evenly over rolls, leaving a one-inch border. Sprinkle with Parmesan cheese. Roll up dough jelly-roll style, starting with one short edge. Cut into 16 slices. Place slices, cut-side down, on a greased baking sheet. Top each slice with one pepperoni slice and one teaspoon mozzarella cheese. Bake at 375 degrees for 9 to 11 minutes, until edges are golden and cheese is melted. Serve warm. Serves 6 to 8.

Snack time calls for lots of cheese. To grate or shred a block of cheese easily, place the wrapped cheese in the freezer for 10 to 20 minutes...it will glide right across the grater!

Cheesy Bean Dip

*So easy to make...so easy to eat! (Even for a dip like Odie.) Stir in
a few drops of hot pepper sauce if you like your dip extra spicy.*

2 16-oz. cans refried beans
2 8-oz. pkgs. cream cheese,
   softened
1/2 c. shredded Cheddar Jack
   cheese

1/4 c. green onions or black
   olives, sliced
tortilla chips or snack crackers

Spoon beans into a large bowl. With an electric mixer on medium-low
speed, beat in cream cheese until smooth. Spread mixture on a serving
plate. Top with cheese and onions or olives. Cover and chill until
serving time. Serve with chips or crackers. Serves 6 to 8.

A new way to serve your favorite dip! Just spread dip
onto flour tortillas, roll up jelly-roll style and cut
into one-inch slices. Add some kick by topping each
with a jalapeño pepper slice.

SNACK ATTACK!

Liz's Delish Guacamole

To tell if avocados are ripe, give them a gentle squeeze.
They should yield slightly but not be too soft.

2 avocados, halved and pitted
1/3 c. to 1/2 c. medium-hot
   chunky salsa

1 t. lemon or lime juice
salt and pepper to taste
tortilla chips

Scoop avocados into a bowl; mash with a fork to desired consistency. Add salsa, juice, salt and pepper; blend well. Serve immediately, or press plastic wrap directly onto the surface of the guacamole and refrigerate. Serve with tortilla chips. Makes about 1-1/2 cups.

Freeze fresh, mashed avocado to keep on hand for quick guacamole...handy to know when avocados are on sale. Just add 1/2 teaspoon of lime or lemon juice per avocado, mix well and store in a plastic zipping bag, making sure to press out all the air before sealing. Thaw in the refrigerator before using.

Hot & Sticky Buffalo Wings

*Bring on the blue cheese dressing and celery sticks...
treat your mouth to some fun!*

3 lbs. chicken wings
seasoned salt to taste
2-oz. bottle hot pepper sauce

1 c. water
1 c. brown sugar, packed
1 T. mustard seed

Arrange chicken wings on a lightly greased 15"x10" jelly-roll pan.
Bake, uncovered, at 400 degrees for 20 minutes. Turn wings over.
Bake for an additional 20 to 30 minutes, until wings are golden and
juices run clear. Drain; arrange on a serving platter and sprinkle with
seasoned salt. Combine remaining ingredients in a saucepan over
medium heat. Bring to a boil; reduce heat to low. Simmer, stirring
occasionally, until sauce turns a dark burgundy color. Drizzle sauce
over wings, or serve on the side for dipping. Makes about 3 dozen.

Spicy Honey Chicken Wings

*Alongside sticky foods, set out a basket of rolled-up napkins,
moistened with warm lemon-scented water. Very thoughtful!*

3 lbs. chicken wings
1/2 c. chili sauce
1 T. honey

1 T. soy sauce
1/2 t. dry mustard
1/4 t. cayenne pepper

Place chicken wings in a greased 3-quart casserole dish. Combine
remaining ingredients in a small bowl; stir well. Drizzle mixture over
wings and toss to coat. Cover and refrigerate for one hour. Uncover and
bake at 350 degrees for 45 to 60 minutes, gently turning once or twice,
until wings are golden and juices run clear. Makes about 3 dozen.

Party fun for all ages...serve finger foods on a paper plate
tucked inside a plastic flying disc for each person.

SNACK ATTACK!

Chef's Surprise Tangy Meatballs

Your friends will never guess what gives these meatballs their delicious flavor. Shhh...it's chili sauce and grape jelly, but we won't tell if you don't!

2 lbs. ground beef
2 eggs, beaten
1/2 t. salt
3/4 c. quick-cooking oats,
   uncooked

1-1/3 c. chili sauce, divided
1/2 c. grape jelly

In a large bowl, combine beef, eggs, salt, oats and 1/3 cup chili sauce. Mix well with your hands; form into one-inch balls. Place in an ungreased shallow 13"x9" baking pan. Bake, uncovered, at 400 degrees for 15 to 17 minutes, until meatballs are browned; drain. Meanwhile, combine jelly and remaining sauce in a large saucepan over medium heat. Cover and cook, stirring occasionally, for about 10 minutes, until mixture is well blended. Add meatballs; simmer until heated through. Meatballs may be kept warm in a slow cooker while serving. Makes about 5 dozen.

Making lots of meatballs? Grab a melon baller and start scooping...you'll be done in record time!

77

Heavenly Herb Dip

*Keep a pair of kitchen scissors handy for snipping fresh herbs,
chopping bacon and opening packages...you'll wonder
how you ever got along without them!*

1 cucumber, peeled and coarsely
   chopped
1 red onion, chopped
2 4-oz. containers crumbled
   feta cheese

1 T. olive oil
2-1/2 T. lemon juice
3 T. fresh dill, chopped
3 T. fresh mint, chopped
Garnish: fresh mint sprigs

Combine cucumber, onion and cheese in a bowl. Sprinkle with oil, juice
and herbs; toss to mix. Cover and chill until serving time. Garnish with
mint sprigs. Serve with Homemade Pita Chips. Makes 6 servings.

Homemade Pita Chips:

3 pita rounds
3 T. olive oil

1/4 t. salt
1/4 t. pepper

Split pita rounds in half; cut each round into 8 wedges. Brush oil over
both sides of wedges; sprinkle with salt and pepper. Arrange wedges in
a single layer on a lightly greased baking sheet. Bake at 375 degrees
for 6 minutes on each side, or until crisp.

Dip to go! Spoon some creamy
vegetable dip into a tall plastic
cup and add crunchy celery
and carrot sticks, red
pepper strips, cucumber
slices and snow pea pods.
Add a lid and the snack is
ready to tote. Be sure to
keep it chilled.

SNACK ATTACK!

Yummy Tuna Spread

For a really low-carb way to enjoy this savory dip, spread it on lettuce leaves and roll up, or spoon onto sweet red pepper strips.

12-oz. can tuna, drained
8-oz. pkg. cream cheese,
   softened
1/2 c. mayonnaise
2 T. onion, finely chopped

1 t. dried parsley
1/2 t. dried chives
1/2 t. hot pepper sauce
1/2 t. pepper
snack crackers or hard rolls

In a bowl, combine all ingredients except crackers or rolls. Beat with an electric mixer on low speed until smooth. Cover and chill until serving time. Serve with crackers as an appetizer spread, or on rolls as a sandwich spread. Makes about 3 cups.

Keep party time super-simple! Serve one or two easy
homemade dishes, and just pick up some tasty go-withs
like pickles, snack crackers and cocktail nuts at
the grocery store.

Savory Snacking Mix

Savor the flavor! Bet you can't stop munching on this crunchy & flavorful mix!

6 c. bite-size crispy corn, wheat and/or rice cereal squares
2 c. doughnut-shaped oat cereal
1 c. plain fish-shaped crackers
1 c. pretzel rings
1 c. pecan halves

2 T. butter, melted
3-1/2 T. Worcestershire sauce
1-1/2 t. seasoned salt
3/4 t. garlic powder
1/2 t. onion powder

In a one-gallon plastic zipping bag, mix together cereals, crackers, pretzels and pecans. In a small bowl, stir together remaining ingredients. Pour butter mixture over cereal mixture; seal bag and shake to coat well. Spread mix onto ungreased baking sheets. Bake at 250 degrees for one hour, stirring every 15 minutes. Let cool; store in an airtight container. Makes 11 cups.

For fun party favors, fill clear plastic cups with crunchy snack mix. Seal with sheets of colorful plastic wrap to keep the goodies inside. Heap the cups in a basket...guests can choose a favorite to take home.

SNACK ATTACK!

Pizza Pretzel Nibblers

Mmm...now you can take along a pizza anywhere you go!
Let the nibbling begin!

2 10-oz. pkgs. sourdough
   pretzel nuggets
1/2 c. canola oil

1 c. grated Parmesan cheese
1-1/4 oz. pkg. spaghetti sauce
   mix

Combine all ingredients in a large bowl; toss to coat nuggets well.
Spread nuggets on an aluminum foil-lined baking sheet. Bake at
275 degrees for 45 minutes, stirring occasionally. Let cool; store in an
airtight container. Makes 6 to 8 servings.

Sparkling Fruit Punch

Fizzy and refreshing...just the thing to go with salty snacks.

32-oz. bottle cranberry juice
   cocktail
32-oz. bottle pineapple juice

1-1/2 c. sugar, or to taste
2-ltr. bottle ginger ale, chilled

In a large pitcher, combine juices and sugar. Stir well until sugar
dissolves. Cover and chill. Add ginger ale just before serving. Makes
one gallon.

Nestle stemmed glasses in ice until
serving time. Frosty glasses make
cold drinks extra tasty!

Hot Cheddar Fondue

Nothing's better than Cheddar! Fill a basket with all kinds of cubed bread for dipping. Sourdough, rustic white and pumpernickel are delicious. Try bread sticks and pretzel rods too!

1/4 c. butter
1/4 c. all-purpose flour
1/2 t. salt
1/4 t. pepper
1/4 t. mustard

1/4 t. Worcestershire sauce
1-1/2 c. milk
8-oz. pkg. shredded Cheddar
   cheese
bread cubes

Melt butter in a large saucepan over medium-high heat. Add flour, salt, pepper, mustard and Worcestershire sauce; whisk until smooth. Gradually stir in milk; bring to a boil. Cook and stir for 2 minutes, or until thickened. Reduce heat to low; add cheese and stir until melted. Transfer mixture to a fondue pot or slow cooker; keep warm. Serve with bread cubes for dipping. Makes 2-1/2 cups.

Chocolate fondue that's out of this world! Melt together 24 ounces semi-sweet chocolate chips, 6 tablespoons corn syrup and one pint whipping cream. Serve with strawberries, fruit cubes and vanilla wafers for dipping.

SNACK ATTACK!

Wonderful Warm Corn Dip

Instant party! With four cans of veggies and a block of cream cheese, you can serve up this bowl of goodness on a moment's notice. Enjoy!

8-oz. pkg. cream cheese,
    softened
15-1/4 oz. can yellow corn,
    drained
15-oz. can shoepeg corn,
    drained
10-oz. can diced tomatoes with
    green chiles, drained

2 t. chili powder
2 t. ground cumin
1 t. garlic powder
salt to taste
corn or tortilla chips

In a microwave-safe bowl, mix together all ingredients except chips. Microwave, uncovered, on high until heated through and cheese is melted, 2 to 3 minutes. Stir to blend. Serve warm with chips. Makes 8 to 12 servings.

Paper coffee filters are wonderful party kitchen helpers! Fill them with popcorn or potato chips... use them as no-drip holders for hot dogs or tacos. They can even be placed over food being reheated in the microwave to cut down on spattering.

Super Snack Mix

This crunchy mix is equally good for carrying along on nature hikes and for lazy munching in front of the TV...can't beat that!

2 c. cheese-flavored fish-shaped
    crackers
2 c. doughnut-shaped oat cereal

1/2 c. dried cranberries
1/2 c. candy corn

Combine all ingredients in a plastic zipping bag. Seal bag and shake to mix. Makes 5 cups.

Yummy Spiders

Defeat Garfield's arch-enemies by gobbling them up! Kids love to make these clever snacks...they're perfect for after school.

creamy peanut butter
buttery round crackers
pretzel sticks

sweetened dried cranberries or
    mini chocolate chips

For each spider, spread a little peanut butter on a cracker and add 4 pretzel sticks on each side for legs. Spread peanut butter on another cracker and press together gently. Stick on cranberry or chocolate chip eyes with a little more peanut butter. Make as many as you like!

SNACK ATTACK!

Peanut Butter People Chow

Irresistible! This recipe makes ten cups, but it should say "one serving"...that's how delicious it is! Send home any leftovers in doggie bags.

9 c. bite-size crispy corn or
    rice cereal squares
1 c. semi-sweet chocolate chips
2 c. creamy peanut butter

1/4 c. butter
1 t. vanilla extract
1-1/2 c. powdered sugar

Place cereal in a large bowl; set aside. Combine chocolate chips, peanut butter and butter in a microwave-safe bowl. Microwave on high, uncovered, for one minute; stir. Microwave an additional 30 seconds stir again until smooth. Blend in vanilla. Pour mixture over cereal; stir until cereal is coated. Let stand until chocolate is set. Pour into a large plastic zipping bag. Add powdered sugar and shake until well coated. Seal bag to store. Makes 10 cups.

WILL EAT HOMEWORK FOR FOOD

Send a big plastic zipping bag filled with People Chow and a copy of Garfield's latest comic book to your favorite college student...a welcome gift anytime!

Dreamy Hot Artichoke Dip

Veggies have never tasted so good!

2 6-oz. cans marinated
  artichokes, drained and
  coarsely chopped
1/2 c. mayonnaise
1-1/2 c. shredded Parmesan
  cheese
1-1/2 c. shredded mozzarella
  cheese

8-oz. pkg. cream cheese,
  softened
1/2 onion, chopped
2 cloves garlic, pressed
salt and pepper to taste
Optional: 1-1/2 t. prepared
  horseradish
shredded wheat crackers

In a large bowl, combine all ingredients except crackers. Mix well;
spread in a lightly greased 13"x9" baking pan. Bake, uncovered, at
350 degrees for 45 minutes, or until golden and bubbly. Serve warm
with crackers. Makes about 6 cups.

Host an old-fashioned game night. All you need are a stack
of favorite board games and some yummy snacks. Pick up
some crazy prizes from the dollar store...fun for all ages!

SNACK ATTACK!

Sweet Onion Dip

Place onions in the freezer for five minutes before slicing them...no more tears!

2 c. sweet onion, diced
2 c. mayonnaise

2 c. shredded Swiss cheese
snack crackers

Stir together onion, mayonnaise and cheese in a bowl. Spread in a lightly greased 8"x8" baking pan. Bake, uncovered, at 350 degrees for 20 minutes, until bubbly and golden. Serve warm with crackers. Makes 6 cups.

Cool & Creamy Green Onion Dip

Use reduced-fat cream cheese, mayonnaise and milk for a no-guilt version of this scrumptious dip.

2 8-oz. pkgs. cream cheese, softened
1 c. mayonnaise
1/2 c. milk

1/2 t. Worcestershire sauce
2 bunches green onions, chopped
snack crackers

Combine cream cheese and mayonnaise in a bowl; mix until well blended. Add milk and Worcestershire sauce; blend well. Stir in onions. Cover and refrigerate for 3 hours, to allow flavors to blend. Serve with crackers. Makes about 4 cups.

A tasty snack in seconds! Wrap thin slices of baked ham and Muenster cheese around well-drained artichoke quarters, place on top of toasty bread rounds and broil until cheese begins to melt.

Cut calories and fat without giving up flavor!

- Dollop spicy salsa on breakfast eggs, baked potatoes, grilled chicken, burgers, even salads.

- Use non-stick vegetable spray to grease skillets and baking pans.

- Try reduced-fat sour cream, cream cheese and mayonnaise in your favorite recipes...replace sour cream with low-fat plain Greek yogurt.

- Jazz up plain foods with fresh herbs like basil, parsley, thyme, chives and mint.

Reduced-fat cheeses won't toughen if added to a hot skillet dish or casserole after it's cooked.

Snack on crunchy baby carrots and sweet red pepper strips dunked in low-fat ranch salad dressing.

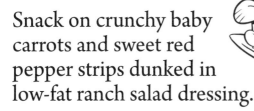

Air-popped popcorn is filling and healthy! Sprinkle it with grated Parmesan cheese for extra flavor.

For dessert, treat yourself to juicy strawberries or sliced peaches topped with creamy vanilla yogurt.

Pull-Apart Pizza Bread

*Another fun-to-eat way to enjoy one of Garfield's
all-time favorite foods!*

12-oz. tube refrigerated flaky
    biscuits
1 T. olive oil
12 slices pepperoni, quartered
1 onion, chopped

1/4 c. shredded pizza-blend
    cheese
1/4 c. grated Parmesan cheese
1 t. Italian seasoning
1/4 t. garlic salt

Cut each biscuit into 4 pieces; place in a bowl. Toss biscuit pieces with
oil and set aside. In a separate bowl, combine remaining ingredients;
mix well. Add biscuits; toss well to coat. Arrange in a Bundt® pan lined
with well-greased aluminum foil. Bake at 400 degrees for 15 minutes,
or until golden. Turn bread out of pan onto a serving plate while still
warm. Makes about 2 dozen pieces.

Super-simple cheese snacks! Cut several 8-ounce packages
of cream cheese into 10 cubes each. Shape cubes into
balls and roll in finely chopped pecans or snipped
fresh parsley. Arrange on a plate, cover and
pop in the fridge until party time.

SNACK ATTACK!

English Muffin Mini Pizzas

It's OK to play with your food! Use pepperoni slices, olives, strips of pepper and other toppings to make funny faces on your little pizzas.

12-oz. pkg. English muffins, split
15-oz. can pizza sauce

2 c. shredded mozzarella cheese
Optional: pepperoni slices

Place muffin halves on an ungreased baking sheet, cut-side up. Spread each with pizza sauce; sprinkle with cheese. If desired, top each muffin half with several pepperoni slices. Bake at 350 degrees for 10 minutes, or until edges are toasty and cheese is melted. Makes 6 servings of 2 muffin halves each.

A quick and tasty appetizer in an instant...place a block of cream cheese on a serving plate, spoon sweet-hot pepper jelly over it and serve with crisp crackers. Works great with fruit chutney or spicy salsa too!

Baked Chile Rellenos

Poppers in a pan...so much easier than
filling individual peppers!

2 8-oz. cans whole green chiles, drained
1 lb. Monterey Jack cheese, sliced
6 eggs, beaten

1-1/2 c. all-purpose flour
2 c. milk
3 T. shortening, melted and slightly cooled
1/4 t. salt

Layer chiles and cheese slices in a greased 13"x9" baking pan. In a bowl, whisk together eggs, flour, milk, shortening and salt; pour over cheese. Bake, uncovered, at 350 degrees for 30 minutes, or until golden. Cut into squares; serve warm. Serves 6 to 8.

Safety first! Always wear plastic gloves to protect your hands when working with hot peppers, and make sure you don't touch your face or eyes.

SNACK ATTACK!

Easy Cheesy Chili Dip

Put some yummy in your tummy!

1 c. onion, chopped
2 T. butter
10-3/4 oz. can cream of
   mushroom soup

15-oz. can chili without beans
8-oz. pkg. shredded Cheddar
   cheese
tortilla chips

In a large saucepan over medium heat, cook onion in butter until tender, about 5 minutes. Stir in soup, chili and cheese. Reduce heat to low. Cook, stirring occasionally, until bubbly and cheese is melted. Serve warm with tortilla chips. Makes about 5 cups.

Simple Summer Salsa

Enjoy this fresh salsa anytime...roma tomatoes and red onions are available year 'round. Fresh parsley may be substituted for some of the cilantro.

10 roma tomatoes, chopped
1/2 c. red onion, chopped
1 c. fresh cilantro, chopped
1 T. cider vinegar

1/2 c. olive oil
juice of 2 Key limes
tortilla chips

Combine all ingredients except chips in a bowl; stir to blend. Cover and refrigerate until chilled. Serve with tortilla chips. Makes about 3 cups.

No one can resist fresh salsa and chips! Pile blue and yellow tortilla chips in a colorful bowl, placed in the middle of a large platter. Add a bowl of tangy salsa... what could be quicker?

Mexi-Corny Popcorn Shake

*For a quick & easy snack that everybody loves, nothing beats
a big bowl of fresh-popped popcorn! It's showtime!*

2 T. chili powder   1 T. garlic powder
2 T. dried parsley   1 t. red pepper flakes
2 T. ground cumin   1 t. salt
1 T. onion powder

Combine all ingredients in a small bowl; stir well. Store in an airtight
container with a shaker top. Sprinkle to taste over hot buttered
popcorn. Makes about 1/2 cup.

Pizzeria Popcorn Sprinkle

This seasoning will make your tongue jump for joy!

1/4 c. grated Parmesan cheese   2 t. paprika
2 t. garlic powder   1 t. salt
2 t. Italian seasoning   2 t. pepper

Place all ingredients in a blender. Process about 30 seconds, until
finely ground. Store in an airtight container with a shaker top. Sprinkle
to taste over hot buttered popcorn. Makes about 1/2 cup.

Need a quick gift for a
friend? Fill a new paper paint
bucket with a jar of popcorn
seasoning, a box of microwave
popcorn and a DVD of a
favorite movie. Decorate with
stickers. Sure to be a big hit!

SNACK ATTACK!

Salty-Sweet Crunchy Mix

Monstrously delicious and fun! Use any combo of favorite crunchy cereals and small crackers. Add candies in colors for your special occasion...team colors for tailgating, red & green for Christmas.

9 c. cereal and/or small plain
   crackers
4 c. popped popcorn
1-1/2 c. dry-roasted peanuts
1/2 c. butter

1/2 c. light corn syrup
1 c. brown sugar, packed
1 t. vanilla extract
1/2 t. baking soda
2 c. candy-coated chocolates

In a lightly greased large roasting pan, mix cereal or crackers, popcorn and peanuts; set aside. In a saucepan over medium heat, stir together butter, corn syrup and brown sugar. Bring to a boil. Boil without stirring for 5 minutes. Remove pan from heat. Stir in vanilla and baking soda. Pour butter mixture over cereal mixture; toss to coat. Bake, uncovered, at 250 degrees for 45 minutes, stirring every 15 minutes. Let cool completely. Add chocolates and toss to mix. Store in an airtight container. Makes about 18 cups.

Peanuts are yummy in crunchy snack mixes, but if you need to avoid them, here are some tasty substitutes to try: dried fruit bits, sunflower kernels and mini pretzel twists. Or, just omit the nuts...your snack mix will still be tasty.

Best-Ever Sausage Balls

The baked sausage balls can be cooled and frozen, then reheated later...equally handy for surprise guests and for midnight snacking.

16-oz. pkg. hot ground pork
   sausage
2 c. biscuit baking mix

3 c. shredded sharp Cheddar
   cheese

In a large bowl, combine uncooked sausage and biscuit mix; mix well using your hands. Add cheese; mix well. Form into walnut-sized balls, pressing together firmly. Arrange balls on lightly greased baking sheets. Bake at 400 degrees for about 20 minutes, until golden and cooked through. Serve warm. Makes 3 to 4 dozen.

ONE GOOD MEAL DESERVES
ANOTHER

Snackers will eat up fresh veggies like baby carrots, celery sticks, cherry tomatoes and broccoli flowerets if they're served with a creamy dill dip! Combine one cup reduced-fat sour cream, 1/2 cup reduced-fat mayonnaise, 2 teaspoons dill weed and 2 teaspoons lemon juice. Chill for several hours before serving.

SNACK ATTACK!

Crispy Bacon Bread Sticks

*Bacon, bread and cheese...this taste-tempting trio
is a welcome addition to any party tray!*

1 c. grated Parmesan cheese
2 t. garlic salt
12 slices bacon, halved

24 4-1/2 inch sesame bread
sticks

Mix cheese and garlic salt in a shallow bowl; set aside. Wrap a
half-slice of bacon around each bread stick, starting at one end and
spiraling to the other end. Arrange bread sticks on a parchment paper-
lined baking sheet. Bake at 350 degrees for 15 minutes, or until bacon
is crisp. Remove from oven; immediately roll bread sticks in cheese
mixture. Let cool before serving. Makes 2 dozen.

Mmm...is anything better than
bacon? To separate bacon slices
easily, first let the package
stand at room temperature
for about 20 minutes.

Cool Peach Smoothie

*Freeze large green seedless grapes to use as fruity ice cubes...
fun to eat when you finish the beverage!*

2 c. ripe peaches, pitted, sliced
  and frozen
1/4 c. frozen orange juice
  concentrate

2 c. milk
1 T. sugar, or to taste
1/4 t. vanilla extract
5 to 6 ice cubes

Combine all ingredients in a blender; process until smooth. Pour into
glasses; serve immediately. Makes 4 servings.

Strawberry-Orange Shake

Garnish with a whole strawberry, orange wedge or mint sprig.

10-oz. pkg. frozen sliced
  strawberries, partially
  thawed
2 c. orange juice

1/2 c. milk
1-1/2 t. sugar
4 to 6 ice cubes

Combine strawberries, orange juice, milk and sugar in a blender;
process until smooth. Add ice cubes; process again until smooth. Pour
into glasses; serve immediately. Makes 4 servings.

Fruit-filled smoothies are
delicious and good for you!
Try using regular or low-fat
milk, soy milk, almond milk
or coconut milk...there's sure
to be one that suits you.

SNACK ATTACK!

Banana-Berry Smoothie

Sweeten with a spoonful of honey, if you like.

1 ripe banana, cut into chunks
1/2 c. blueberries
1 c. low-fat vanilla yogurt
1 c. milk
2 T. ground flaxseed
Optional: 3 to 4 ice cubes

Combine all ingredients in a blender; process until smooth. Pour into glasses; serve immediately. Makes 3 to 4 servings.

Chocolatey Moo Cow Shake

Add a candy-striped drinking straw just for fun!

2 c. milk
1 scoop vanilla ice cream
1 scoop chocolate ice cream
3 T. chocolate syrup
Optional: crushed ice

Combine all ingredients except ice in a blender; process until smooth. Pour into 2 glasses, over ice, if desired. Serve immediately. Makes 2 servings.

For a sweet & salty snack that's ready in minutes, serve a tub of caramel apple dip with crunchy apple slices and mini pretzel twists. Yum...dig in!

Almond Toffee Popcorn

Yum! Nothing beats homemade caramel corn for munching and sharing with friends.

12 c. popped popcorn
1 c. sugar
1/2 c. butter
1/2 c. light corn syrup

1/4 c. water
1 c. toasted almonds, chopped
1/2 t. vanilla extract

Place popcorn in a large heat-proof bowl; remove any unpopped kernels and set aside. In a large saucepan, combine remaining ingredients except vanilla. Cook over medium-high heat, stirring constantly, until mixture reaches the soft-crack stage, or 270 to 289 degrees on a candy thermometer. Remove from heat; add vanilla and stir well. Pour over popcorn, mixing until coated. Spread on wax paper to dry. Store in an airtight container. Makes about 12 cups.

Save the plastic liners when you toss out empty cereal boxes. They're perfect for storing homemade snack mixes and baked goodies.

SNACK ATTACK!

Sweet Rainbow Popcorn

Use any color of food coloring you like...how about orange for our favorite cat? If you want to make several different colors, divide the hot popcorn mixture into bowls, then stir in the food coloring.

8 c. popped popcorn
2 c. sugar
1/2 c. milk

1 t. vanilla extract
3 to 6 drops desired food
    coloring

Place popcorn in a large roasting pan; remove any unpopped kernels and set aside. In a heavy saucepan over medium heat, combine sugar and milk. Bring to a boil. Boil and stir for about 22 minutes, until mixture reaches the soft-ball stage, or 234 to 243 degrees on a candy thermometer. Remove pan from heat. Stir in vanilla and food coloring; mix well. Pour sugar mixture over popcorn. Stir well to coat popcorn evenly. Spread popcorn on wax paper to dry. If popcorn remains sticky, bake it at 300 degrees for 5 to 10 minutes. Store in an airtight container. Makes about 8 cups.

Serve party popcorn or snack mix in a big bowl along with a scoop. A stack of lunch-size paper bags nearby will make it easy for everyone to help themselves.

Garfield's Tuna Treats *(for real cats)*

Doesn't your favorite feline friend deserve some fishy goodies?

2 5-oz. cans tuna, drained and flaked
1 egg, beaten
1-1/2 t. oil

1-1/2 c. soft whole-grain bread crumbs
Optional: 1/2 t. brewer's yeast

Combine all ingredients in a bowl; mix with a fork. Drop by 1/4 teaspoonfuls onto greased baking sheets. Bake at 350 degrees for 8 minutes. Cool. Store, refrigerated, in an airtight container. Makes 7 to 8 dozen.

Odie's Sit Up & Beg Biscuits *(for real dogs)*

Your dog will flip for these home-baked biscuits!

2 c. whole-wheat flour
3/4 c. all-purpose flour
1/3 c. cornmeal
1/4 c. quick-cooking oats, uncooked

1/2 t. salt
2 eggs, beaten
1/2 c. milk
1/4 c. molasses
2 T. oil

Mix flours, cornmeal, oats and salt in a large bowl. Add remaining ingredients; stir until a soft dough forms. Roll out dough, 1/2-inch thick, on a well-floured surface. Cut out biscuits with a cookie cutter. Arrange on a greased baking sheet. Bake at 350 degrees for 30 minutes, then turn off oven. Leave biscuits in the oven for another 20 minutes to harden. Cool. Store in an airtight container. Makes about one dozen.

How does Garfield love lasagna?
Let us count the ways!

LOTSA LASAGNA, PASTA & PIZZA

Classic Lasagna

According to Garfield, lasagna is "nature's most perfect food."
A classic recipe...and classics are always in style!

10-oz. pkg. lasagna noodles,
   uncooked
1/2 lb. ground beef
1/2 lb. ground Italian pork
   sausage
1 onion, diced
1 clove garlic, minced
14-1/2 oz. can Italian-seasoned
   stewed tomatoes

2 6-oz. cans tomato paste
2 T. Italian seasoning
3 c. ricotta cheese
1/2 c. grated Parmesan cheese
2 eggs, beaten
2 T. dried parsley
salt and pepper to taste
16-oz. pkg. shredded mozzarella
   cheese, divided

Cook noodles according to package directions; drain. Meanwhile, in a skillet over medium heat, brown beef, sausage and onion; drain. Add garlic, undrained tomatoes, tomato paste and Italian seasoning; simmer for about 10 minutes. In a large bowl, blend together ricotta and Parmesan cheeses, eggs and seasonings. Spread 1/2 cup of beef mixture in a lightly greased deep 13"x9" baking pan. Layer as follows: 1/3 each of noodles, cheese mixture, beef mixture and mozzarella cheese. Repeat layers, ending with mozzarella. Cover with aluminum foil. Bake at 350 degrees for 45 minutes to one hour, until hot and bubbly. Let stand for 10 minutes before slicing. Serves 6 to 8.

"Cook" lasagna noodles the lazy way! Put them in a baking pan filled with very hot water while mixing up the rest of the recipe. They will be soft and pliable when you're ready for them!

Bachelor-Style Skillet Lasagna

All the flavor of baked lasagna, but ready to enjoy in 30 minutes. Life is short...eat now!

1 lb. ground turkey or beef
2 14-oz. cans beef broth
14-1/2 oz. can diced tomatoes
1/4 t. Italian seasoning
1/4 t. garlic powder

2 c. rotini pasta, uncooked
1/2 c. shredded mozzarella
   cheese
Garnish: grated Parmesan
   cheese

Brown meat in a skillet over medium heat; drain. Stir in broth, undrained tomatoes and seasonings; bring to a boil. Stir in uncooked pasta. Cover and simmer for 12 to 14 minutes, until pasta is tender. Stir in mozzarella cheese. Top with Parmesan cheese. Serves 4.

Buttery Garlic Bread

A must with lasagna! Perfect for jazzing up leftover hot dog buns.

1/2 c. butter, softened
2 T. mayonnaise
3 cloves garlic, chopped
2 t. dried oregano
1/4 t. dried sage

1 t. salt
1 t. pepper
1 loaf Italian bread, halved
   lengthwise
2 T. grated Parmesan cheese

Combine all ingredients except bread and cheese in a bowl. Place bread, cut-side up, on an ungreased baking sheet. Spread evenly with butter mixture; sprinkle with cheese. Place bread 4 inches under a heated broiler. Broil for 5 minutes, or until lightly toasted. Serves 6.

Read the recipe the whole way through and make sure you have everything you'll need before you start cooking.

LOTSA LASAGNA, PASTA & PIZZA

Bow-Tie Lasagna

If you're a fraidy cat in the kitchen, you'll find these bow ties are easier to handle than lasagna noodles...but just as yummy!

2-1/4 c. bow-tie pasta, uncooked
1/2 lb. ground beef
1/2 lb. ground Italian pork
   sausage
1/2 c. onion, chopped
15-oz. can pizza sauce

1/2 t. salt
1/8 t. garlic powder
8-oz. container cottage cheese
8-oz. pkg. shredded mozzarella
   cheese

Cook pasta according to package directions; drain. Meanwhile, in a skillet over medium heat, brown beef, sausage and onion; drain. Stir in pizza sauce and seasonings; simmer until heated through. Stir in cooked pasta and cottage cheese. Spoon into a lightly greased 2-quart casserole dish; top with mozzarella cheese. Bake, uncovered, at 350 degrees for 20 to 25 minutes, until hot and bubbly. Serves 6.

LASAGNA...NATURE'S PERFECT FOOD

The secret to perfect pasta! Fill a big pot with water and bring it to a rolling boil. Add a tablespoon of salt. Stir in pasta; bring back to a rolling boil. Boil, uncovered, for the time given on the package. You don't need to add oil...stir often, and the pasta won't stick together.

Emergency Lasagna

Scrumptious...and a snap to put together!

26-oz. jar spaghetti sauce,
    divided
20-oz. pkg. refrigerated cheese
    ravioli, uncooked and divided
10-oz. pkg. frozen chopped
    spinach, thawed, drained
    and divided

8-oz. pkg. shredded mozzarella
    cheese, divided
1/2 c. grated Parmesan cheese,
    divided

Spread 1/2 cup sauce in a lightly greased 9"x9" baking pan. Layer half of the ravioli, half of the spinach, half of each cheese and 1/3 of remaining sauce. Repeat layers, ending with cheeses. Cover with aluminum foil. Bake at 350 degrees for 25 minutes. Uncover; bake an additional 10 minutes. Let stand several minutes before serving. Serves 4 to 6.

Easy-Peasy Mushroom Lasagna

...because you really can't have too many lasagna recipes!

16-oz. pkg. lasagna noodles,
    uncooked
1 lb. ground beef
28-oz. jar spaghetti sauce
4-oz. can sliced mushrooms,
    drained

3 c. shredded Italian-blend
    cheese, divided
1/4 c. grated Parmesan cheese

Cook noodles according to package directions; drain. Meanwhile, brown beef in a skillet over medium heat; drain. Add sauce and mushrooms; simmer for 3 minutes. Spread a thin layer of sauce mixture in a lightly greased 13"x9" baking pan. Layer with 1/3 each of noodles and shredded cheese. Repeat layers, ending with cheese. Sprinkle Parmesan cheese on top. Bake, uncovered, at 350 degrees for 45 minutes, or until hot and bubbly. Let stand for 10 minutes before slicing. Serves 6 to 8.

Cheesy Lasagna Rolls

It's hard to believe anyone could get bored with lasagna.
But if you are, here's a new trick...teach the noodles to roll over!

12-oz. pkg. lasagna noodles,
    uncooked
1 lb. ground pork sausage
1 green pepper, diced
8-oz. pkg. cream cheese,
    softened
3-oz. pkg. cream cheese,
    softened

1 bunch green onions,
    chopped
28-oz. jar spaghetti sauce,
    divided
1-1/2 c. shredded mozzarella
    cheese

Cook noodles just until tender; remove from heat but do not drain. Meanwhile, brown sausage and pepper in a large skillet over medium heat; drain. Add both packages of cream cheese to skillet; stir over low heat until melted. Stir in onions; remove from heat. Spread half of spaghetti sauce in a lightly greased 13"x9" baking pan; set aside. Lay noodles flat, one at a time; spoon one to 2 tablespoons sausage mixture at one end. Carefully roll up noodle; place in baking pan, seam-side down. Repeat with remaining noodles. Top with remaining sauce; sprinkle with cheese. Bake, uncovered, at 350 degrees for 15 to 20 minutes, until bubbly and cheese has melted. Makes 6 servings.

There's no need to rinse pasta after cooking if it will
be served immediately in a hot dish. Unrinsed pasta
holds the sauce much better.

Busy-Day Lasagna Toss

Another scrumptious skillet lasagna...and you don't even have to pre-cook the noodles!

1 lb. ground beef
1 c. green pepper, chopped
1/2 c. onion, chopped
3 cloves garlic, minced
26-oz. jar spaghetti sauce
1-2/3 c. water

1/4 c. Italian salad dressing
1/4 c. brown sugar, packed
12 no-boil lasagna noodles, uncooked
Optional: 1/2 c. ricotta cheese
1 c. shredded mozzarella cheese

Brown beef in a large deep skillet over medium heat; drain. Add pepper, onion and garlic; sauté until tender. Stir in sauce, water, salad dressing and brown sugar; bring to a boil. Break each noodle into 4 pieces. Stir noodles into mixture in skillet; reduce heat to medium-low. Cover and cook, stirring occasionally, until noodles are tender, about 10 to 15 minutes. Remove from heat. Stir in ricotta cheese, if using. Sprinkle with mozzarella cheese; cover. Let stand for about 5 minutes, until cheese is melted. Serves 6.

When a recipe calls for spaghetti sauce, try a new flavor each time! With so many flavorful choices at the grocery store, try swapping out your usual sauce for tomato & basil, roasted red pepper or garlic & herb...the list goes on & on!

Easy Overnight Lasagna

So easy, you don't even have to cook the lasagna noodles! Be sure to cover the pan tightly with foil and allow enough time in the fridge.

1 lb. ground Italian pork
    sausage
26-oz. jar spaghetti sauce
1 c. water
15-oz. container ricotta cheese
1 egg, beaten
2 T. fresh chives, chopped

1/2 t. dried oregano
8-oz. pkg. lasagna noodles,
    uncooked and divided
16-oz. pkg. shredded mozzarella
    cheese, divided
2 T. grated Parmesan cheese

Brown sausage in a skillet over medium heat; drain. Stir in sauce and water; simmer over low heat for 5 minutes. In a bowl, stir together ricotta cheese, egg and herbs; set aside. Spread 1-1/2 cups sausage mixture in the bottom of a lightly greased 13"x9" baking pan. Layer with half of the uncooked noodles, half of the ricotta mixture and half of the mozzarella cheese. Top with remaining sausage mixture; sprinkle with Parmesan cheese. Cover tightly with aluminum foil; refrigerate for 8 hours to overnight. Uncover; bake at 350 degrees for 50 minutes to one hour, until noodles are tender. Cover with foil; let stand 15 minutes before serving. Serves 6.

Cut leftover baked lasagna into serving-size portions and freeze them on a baking sheet, then pack frozen portions in a freezer bag. Later you'll be able to heat up just the number of servings you want.

Creamy Chicken Lasagna

Pick up a juicy rotisserie chicken from the deli to get a head start on this luscious lasagna.

6 to 9 lasagna noodles, uncooked
8-oz. pkg. shredded mozzarella cheese, divided
2 to 3 c. cooked chicken, diced
1 c. onion, finely chopped
1 c. sliced mushrooms
1/4 c. chopped pimentos
1/2 t. garlic powder
8-oz. container sour cream
10-3/4 oz. can cream of chicken soup
10-3/4 oz. cream of mushroom soup
1/2 c. grated Parmesan cheese

Cook noodles according to package directions; drain. In a large bowl, combine 1/2 cup mozzarella cheese and remaining ingredients; stir well. In a lightly greased 13"x9" baking pan, layer half of chicken mixture and half of noodles. Repeat layers; top with remaining mozzarella cheese. Bake, uncovered, at 350 degrees for 40 to 45 minutes, until hot and bubbly. Let stand for 5 to 10 minutes before slicing. Serves 6 to 8.

LASAGNA...THERE'S NO LOVE LIKE YOUR FIRST LOVE

Garlic Vinaigrette Dressing

Even houseplants would taste good topped with this dressing!

1/3 c. olive oil
1/3 c. white wine vinegar
2 cloves garlic, minced
1 T. sugar
1/2 t. salt
1/8 t. pepper

Combine all ingredients in a small jar with a tight-fitting lid. Secure lid; shake vigorously to blend. Keep refrigerated up to 2 weeks. Makes 2/3 cup.

Tex-Mex Chicken Lasagna

Food with a 'tude! Send your taste buds south of the border with this spicy twist on lasagna.

1 onion, chopped
2 cloves garlic, chopped
1 T. olive oil
16-oz. jar salsa
15-oz. can chili with beans
4-oz. can chopped green chiles
2 c. cooked chicken, shredded

1 T. lime juice
1-1/2 t. chili powder
1 t. salt
1/2 t. pepper
9 6-inch flour tortillas, divided
8-oz. pkg. shredded Mexican-
    blend cheese, divided

In a large skillet, cook onion and garlic in oil for 3 to 4 minutes, until onion is tender. Stir in salsa, chili and chiles; reduce heat to low and simmer for several minutes, until heated through. Meanwhile, in a bowl, toss chicken with lime juice and seasonings. Arrange 3 tortillas in the bottom of a lightly greased 13"x9" baking pan. Layer with half of onion mixture, half of chicken mixture and 1/3 of cheese. Repeat layers; top with remaining tortillas and remaining cheese. Bake, uncovered, at 350 degrees for 25 to 30 minutes. Let stand for 5 to 10 minutes before serving. Serves 6.

Set a regular dinner theme for each night and it'll be a snap to make out your shopping list. You'll welcome every Tuesday when you know it's Taco Night!

Ham & Mushroom Tortellini

Creamy, satisfying and fun to eat! If you don't care for peas, just leave 'em out.

9-oz. pkg. refrigerated cheese
   tortellini, uncooked
2 T. butter
1/4 c. red pepper, diced
1 c. sliced mushrooms
3/4 c. milk

1/2 c. water
4 t. cornstarch
1 t. chicken bouillon granules
1 c. cooked ham, cubed
3/4 c. fresh or frozen peas

Cook tortellini according to package directions; drain. Meanwhile, melt butter in a large skillet over medium heat. Add red pepper and mushrooms; cook until tender, about 5 minutes. In a small bowl, combine milk, water, cornstarch and bouillon; stir well. Add milk mixture to skillet. Cook, stirring constantly, until mixture boils and thickens. Stir in ham, peas and tortellini; cook until heated through. Makes 4 servings.

For a delicious, healthy change from pasta, make "noodles" from zucchini and summer squash! Cut squash into long, thin strips or strings, then steam lightly or sauté in a little olive oil. Add your favorite spaghetti sauce and meatballs...yummy!

LOTSA LASAGNA, PASTA & PIZZA

Ravioli & Meatballs Pronto

No-fuss feasting...just five ingredients for a hearty dinner! You'll love it with sliced smoked sausage instead of meatballs too.

25-oz. pkg. frozen cheese-filled ravioli, uncooked
20-oz. pkg. frozen meatballs, thawed

28-oz. jar spaghetti sauce
garlic powder to taste
1-1/2 c. shredded mozzarella cheese

Cook ravioli according to package directions; drain. Place ravioli in a lightly greased 13"x9" baking pan. Top with meatballs and sauce. Sprinkle with garlic powder; top with cheese. Bake, uncovered, at 375 degrees for 35 minutes, or until heated through. Serves 4 to 6.

Angel Hair with Tomato & Basil

If you're lucky enough to have some fresh basil, this simple recipe is a perfect way to enjoy it.

6 to 8 roma tomatoes, diced
1 to 2 cloves garlic, minced
1/2 c. butter, melted
2 T. fresh basil, snipped

8-oz. pkg. angel hair pasta, uncooked
Garnish: shredded Parmesan cheese, fresh basil sprigs

Combine tomatoes and garlic in a saucepan. Simmer over medium-low heat for 10 to 15 minutes. Blend together butter and basil in a bowl; set aside. Cook pasta according to package directions; drain and place in a serving bowl. Top hot pasta with butter mixture; stir in tomato mixture. Garnish as desired. Serves 4.

Keep mini pots of your favorite pizza & pasta herbs like oregano and basil on a sunny kitchen windowsill... right next to the catnip!

A tasty dinner in the freezer is like money in the bank!

Cut leftover lasagna or meatloaf into portions and freeze on a baking sheet, then pack in a plastic freezer bag. Later, heat up as many pieces as you want.

PANT
PANT
PANT
!

Let hot food cool down at least 30 minutes before wrapping & freezing.

Double-wrap casseroles tightly, first in plastic freezer wrap, then in heavy-duty aluminum foil.

Soups freeze well. Ladle into individual plastic containers and freeze...instant lunch!

No more freezer mysteries!
Label each item with
the name and the date.

Wrap up leftover roast beef, chicken or pork in recipe-size portions...easy to thaw, then add to a favorite recipe.

No peeking! Open the freezer door as little as possible to keep fresh taste in, warm air out.

Most home-cooked foods are tastiest if kept frozen no longer than 2 to 3 months.

Mamma's Beef & Sausage Baked Pasta

Straight from the kitchen at Mamma Leoni's where Garfield was born. It's fun to make this hearty casserole with a mix of pastas like ziti, rotini and wagon wheels.

16-oz. pkg. penne pasta,
  uncooked
1 lb. ground beef
1 lb. ground Italian pork
  sausage
1 onion, chopped
2 26-oz. jars spaghetti sauce

8-oz. pkg. shredded provolone
  cheese
8-oz. container sour cream
8-oz. pkg. shredded mozzarella
  cheese
1/2 c. grated Parmesan cheese

Cook pasta according to package directions; drain. Meanwhile, brown beef, sausage and onion in a large skillet over medium heat; drain. Add sauce to skillet and simmer over low heat for 15 minutes. In a greased 13"x9" baking pan, layer half of the pasta, all of the provolone cheese, all of the sour cream, half of the beef mixture, remaining pasta, all of the mozzarella cheese and remaining beef mixture. Top with Parmesan cheese. Bake, uncovered, at 350 degrees for 30 minutes, or until hot and bubbly. Serves 8.

Just making dinner for a few? Divide the ingredients for a large 13"x9" casserole into two smaller 8"x8" pans and freeze one to enjoy later.

LOTSA LASAGNA, PASTA & PIZZA

Stuffed Shells Florentine

*"Florentine" means these saucy shells are stuffed with spinach...
but with all the cheese, Garfield won't even notice!*

12-oz. pkg. jumbo pasta shells,
   uncooked
15-oz. container ricotta cheese
8-oz. pkg. shredded mozzarella
   cheese
1 egg, beaten

10-oz. pkg. frozen chopped
   spinach, thawed and drained
1/2 t. onion powder
1/4 t. nutmeg
28-oz. jar spaghetti sauce

Cook pasta shells according to package directions; drain. Meanwhile, in a large bowl, stir together cheeses, egg, spinach and seasonings. Spoon mixture into shells; arrange shells in a greased 13"x9" baking pan. Spoon sauce over shells. Bake, covered, at 350 degrees for 45 minutes. Serves 6.

Italian Restaurant-Style Bruschetta

Fresh tasting and really easy to fix.

4 to 6 roma tomatoes, diced
3 T. olive oil, divided

1 t. fresh basil, chopped
10 slices Italian bread

In a bowl, combine tomatoes, one tablespoon oil and basil; stir well and set aside. Arrange bread slices in a single layer on an ungreased baking sheet; brush with remaining oil. Place bread about 4 inches below a broiler until lightly golden, about one minute. Top bread with tomato mixture. Makes 10 servings.

Store salad greens in a plastic zipping bag, tucking in
a paper towel to absorb extra moisture. They'll stay
crisp in the refrigerator up to four days.

Chicken & Broccoli Parmesan

Try this creamy stovetop dish with smoked salmon too! It's already cooked, so just flake it, stir it in and heat through.

8-oz. pkg. linguine pasta, uncooked
1 c. broccoli flowerets, cut into bite-size pieces
2 T. butter
1 lb. boneless, skinless chicken breasts, cubed
10-3/4 oz. can cream of mushroom soup
1/2 c. milk
1/2 c. grated Parmesan cheese
1/4 t. pepper

Cook pasta according to package directions. Add broccoli to pasta pot during the last 4 minutes of cooking time; drain. Meanwhile, melt butter in a large deep skillet over medium heat. Add chicken to skillet. Cook until golden and juices run clear when chicken is pierced with a fork. Reduce heat to low. Stir in pasta mixture and remaining ingredients. Simmer for about 5 minutes, until heated through. Serves 4.

Give pasta lots more flavor in a jiffy! Add a bouillon cube or two to the boiling water along with the pasta.

LOTSA LASAGNA, PASTA & PIZZA

Farmers' Market Fettuccine

Cutting up veggies for this recipe? Set aside some extras for lunch tomorrow...enjoy with a dipping cup of ranch salad dressing.

12-oz. pkg. fettuccine pasta, uncooked
1/2 c. creamy Italian salad dressing
1 c. broccoli flowerets, cut into bite-size pieces
1 c. zucchini, sliced
1 c. red pepper, thinly sliced
1/2 c. onion, chopped
1/2 t. dried basil
1/2 c. butter
2 tomatoes, chopped
1/2 c. sliced mushrooms
Garnish: grated Parmesan cheese

Cook pasta according to package directions; drain. Toss warm pasta with salad dressing; stir to coat and set aside. Meanwhile, in a skillet over medium heat, cook broccoli, zucchini, pepper, onion and basil in butter until tender. Stir in tomatoes and mushrooms; cook just until heated through. Toss vegetable mixture with pasta mixture. Garnish with cheese. Serves 6.

Create a cozy Italian restaurant feel for dinner. Toss a red & white checked tablecloth over the table, light drip candles in empty bottles and add a basket of warm garlic bread. Just like Mamma Leoni's!

Good Ol' Spaghetti & Meatballs

Great for a casual dinner with friends. Toss everything together in a big serving bowl and let everyone help themselves!

16-oz. pkg. thin spaghetti,
   uncooked
2 14-1/2 oz. cans diced
   tomatoes
2 6-oz. cans tomato sauce

2/3 c. water
1 t. Italian seasoning
24 meatballs, thawed if frozen
Garnish: grated Parmesan
   cheese

Cook spaghetti according to package directions; drain. Meanwhile, in a saucepan, combine undrained tomatoes, tomato sauce, water and seasoning. Bring to a boil over medium heat; reduce heat and simmer for 5 minutes. Add meatballs; heat through. Ladle sauce and meatballs over cooked spaghetti; sprinkle with cheese. Serves 6.

Sausage & Sweet Pepper Sauce

Equally delicious spooned over pasta or into crusty hard rolls.

1 lb. sweet Italian pork sausage
   links, sliced into thirds
1 T. oil
1 green pepper, diced
1 onion, diced

1 t. garlic, minced
14-1/2 oz. can petite diced
   tomatoes
1 t. dried basil

In a large saucepan over medium-high heat, brown sausage in oil. Reduce heat and cook for 10 minutes; drain and set sausage aside. Add pepper, onion and garlic to pan; stir-fry until tender. Stir in basil. Stir in undrained tomatoes, sausage and basil. Cover and simmer over low heat for about one hour, stirring occasionally, until sausage is no longer pink in the center. Makes 4 servings.

Fill-You-Up Noodle Bake

Whether you call it Johnny Marzetti, Goulash or even American Chop Suey...this is down-home comfort food!

8-oz. pkg. fine egg noodles, uncooked
1 lb. ground beef, browned
29-oz. can tomato sauce
1/2 c. green onions, chopped
8-oz. container sour cream
1 c. cottage cheese
1 t. salt
1/4 t. garlic salt
1/8 t. pepper
1 c. shredded Cheddar cheese

Cook noodles according to package directions; drain. Meanwhile, brown beef in a skillet over medium heat; drain. Stir in remaining ingredients except Cheddar cheese. Gently fold in noodles. Spoon mixture into a lightly greased 2-quart casserole dish. Sprinkle with Cheddar cheese. Bake, uncovered, at 350 degrees for about 30 minutes, or until hot and bubbly. Makes 4 to 6 servings.

Make some tasty noodle patties with leftover spaghetti. Mix 2 to 3 cups cold, cooked pasta with 2 beaten eggs and 1/2 cup ricotta cheese; form into 4 patties. Pan-fry patties in a little olive oil until golden. Serve topped with warm spaghetti sauce...yum!

3-Cheese Spinach Rigatoni

Chock-full of so many good things, you won't miss the meat!

16-oz. pkg. rigatoni pasta,
   uncooked
3 T. olive oil, divided
10-oz. pkg. frozen chopped
   spinach, thawed and drained
16-oz. container ricotta cheese
1/2 t. nutmeg
3/4 t. salt

1/4 t. pepper
5 T. grated Parmesan cheese,
   divided
1-1/2 c. shredded fontina
   cheese, divided
Garnish: grated Parmesan
   cheese

Cook pasta according to package directions. Drain; toss with one
tablespoon oil and place in a greased 13"x9" baking pan. In a food
processor or blender, combine spinach, ricotta cheese, seasonings and
3 tablespoons Parmesan cheese. Process until puréed; stir in 3/4 cup
fontina cheese. Spoon spinach mixture over rigatoni; toss gently to
coat. Sprinkle remaining fontina and Parmesan cheeses over top;
drizzle with remaining oil. Bake, uncovered, at 450 degrees for 15 to
20 minutes, until hot and bubbly. Garnish individual servings with
Parmesan cheese. Serves 4 to 6.

What kind of olive oil to use? "Light" olive oil is fine for
cooking, and it's less expensive. Save extra virgin olive oil
for delicately flavored salad dressings and dipping sauces.

Chicken & Ratatouille Rotini

Add some sliced mushrooms too, if you like.

8-oz. pkg. rotini pasta, uncooked
2 T. olive oil
3/4 lb. boneless, skinless chicken breast, cubed
1 c. green pepper, sliced

1-1/2 c. eggplant, peeled and diced
1-1/2 c. zucchini, thinly sliced
28-oz. jar spaghetti sauce
Garnish: grated Parmesan cheese

Cook pasta according to package directions; drain. Meanwhile, heat oil in a saucepan over medium heat; add chicken and green pepper. Cook and stir until chicken is no longer pink, about 5 minutes. Add eggplant and zucchini. Cook until tender, 3 to 5 minutes; drain. Stir in sauce; bring to a boil. Reduce heat to low. Simmer, uncovered, for about 10 minutes. Ladle sauce over pasta; sprinkle with Parmesan cheese. Serves 6.

Creamy Salmon Manicotti

Pouch-style, canned or smoked salmon all work well in this recipe. You'll need about 1-1/2 cups flaked salmon.

8 manicotti pasta shells, uncooked
2 5-oz. pkgs. pink salmon, flaked

16-oz. container ricotta cheese
1 egg, beaten
15-oz. jar Alfredo sauce
Garnish: dill weed

Cook manicotti shells according to package directions; drain. Meanwhile, remove any bones or skin from salmon. In a bowl, combine salmon, ricotta cheese and egg; mix well. Spoon mixture into shells. Arrange shells in a lightly greased 11"x9" baking pan. Spoon any extra filling around shells. Top with Alfredo sauce; sprinkle with dill weed. Cover and bake at 350 degrees for 35 to 40 minutes, until heated through. Serves 4.

Vito's Deep-Dish Sausage Pizza

With extra everything (in large quantities, if you ask Garfield)!
Add mushrooms, onions, black olives, pepperoni...make it
just the way you like it!

1 loaf frozen bread dough,
   thawed
1 lb. ground Italian pork
   sausage
8-oz. pkg. shredded mozzarella
   cheese
1 green pepper, diced

1 red pepper, diced
28-oz. can diced tomatoes,
   drained
3/4 t. dried oregano
1/4 t. garlic powder
1/2 t. salt
1/2 c. grated Parmesan cheese

Press dough into the bottom and up the sides of a greased 13"x9"
baking pan. Let rise for 10 to 15 minutes. Bake at 400 degrees for
10 minutes. While crust is baking, brown sausage in a skillet over
medium heat; drain. Sprinkle sausage over baked crust; top with
mozzarella cheese. In the same skillet, cook peppers until slightly
tender. Stir in undrained tomatoes and seasonings. Spoon mixture
over pizza. Sprinkle with Parmesan cheese. Bake, uncovered, at
350 degrees for 20 to 25 minutes, until crust is golden. Cut into
squares. Makes 8 servings.

Aged Parmesan cheese is most flavorful when it's freshly
grated. A chunk of Parmesan will stay fresh in the fridge for
several weeks if wrapped in a paper towel dampened with
cider vinegar and then tucked into a plastic zipping bag.

Upside-Down Pizzeria Pot Pie

It's impossible to get bored with pizza...but it's still fun to try it a brand-new way! This is super-simple to make. Even Odie could do it!

1 lb. ground turkey sausage
1/2 c. onion, chopped
1 c. green pepper, chopped
1-1/2 c. sliced mushrooms
Optional: 2 to 3 t. oil

15-oz. can chunky pizza sauce
2 c. biscuit baking mix
1/4 c. milk
1 egg, beaten
2 T. grated Parmesan cheese

In a skillet over medium heat, cook sausage and vegetables until sausage is browned, adding a little oil if needed. Drain; stir in sauce and spoon into an ungreased 3-quart casserole dish. In a bowl, stir together biscuit mix, milk, egg and cheese until a soft dough forms. Turn out onto a floured surface; knead 10 times. Pat dough into a 9-inch circle; cut into 6 wedges. Arrange wedges over sausage mixture. Bake, uncovered, at 400 degrees for about 30 minutes, until filling is bubbly and crust is golden. Makes 6 servings.

Zesty Marinated Olives

Delicious for before-dinner snacking!

6-oz. can whole black olives,
  drained
1/4 c. olive oil
2 T. fresh oregano or basil,
  chopped

1 T. balsamic vinegar
2 cloves garlic, minced
1/2 t. red pepper flakes
1/4 t. salt

Place olives in a wide-mouth glass jar. Add remaining ingredients; close jar and shake gently to mix. Refrigerate at least 2 hours before serving. Keep refrigerated up to 10 days. Makes 8 to 10 servings.

Garlic Chicken Pizza

*Everyone will think you're quite a chef when you serve up this
flavorful pizza packed with fresh ingredients.*

1 T. olive oil
1/2 lb. boneless, skinless
  chicken breasts, cubed
1 clove garlic, minced
1/4 t. fresh basil, chopped
1/4 t. fresh rosemary, chopped
12-inch pre-baked Italian
  pizza crust

15-oz. jar pizza sauce, divided
8-oz. pkg. shredded mozzarella
  cheese
1 to 2 roma tomatoes, sliced
Garnish: grated Romano cheese

Heat oil in a large skillet over medium heat. Sauté chicken with garlic
and herbs until chicken juices run clear; set aside. Place pizza crust on
a lightly greased baking sheet; brush with oil from skillet. Spread crust
with sauce and chicken mixture. Top with mozzarella cheese and
tomato slices. Sprinkle with Romano cheese. Bake at 350 degrees until
cheese bubbles and crust is firm, about 5 minutes. Cut into wedges.
Makes 4 to 6 servings.

Pizza on the grill! Brush a pre-baked pizza crust with
olive oil on both sides. Place crust on a preheated grill. Cook
for 2 to 4 minutes on each side. Top with grilled or sautéed
meat, sliced veggies and shredded cheese. Cook for 8 to
10 minutes more, until the cheese melts.

Double-Crust Pizza Rustica

You'll love this pizza with its rich sausage and cheese filling!

2 9-inch pie crusts
1 lb. ground Italian pork
   sausage
2 T. fennel seed, crushed
6 eggs, beaten
15-oz. container ricotta cheese

8-oz. pkg. shredded mozzarella
   cheese
8-oz. pkg. shredded Muenster
   cheese
1/2 c. shredded Cheddar cheese

Roll out pie crusts to 13"x9" rectangles on a floured surface. Press one crust into the bottom of an ungreased 13"x9" baking pan; set aside. In a skillet over medium heat, brown sausage with fennel seed; drain and let cool slightly. Stir in eggs and cheeses; spread mixture over crust. Top with remaining crust. Cut slits in the top with a knife tip. Bake at 375 degrees for 45 minutes, or until bubbly and crust is golden. Cut into squares. Makes 10 to 15 servings.

Visit a summertime farmers' market for the freshest homegrown pizza toppings! Tomatoes, peppers, onions, garlic, herbs...even farm-made cheese and sausage can be found there. Come early and bring a basket!

French Bread Sausage Pizza

You could microwave a frozen French bread pizza...but why, when it's so easy to make your own fresh-from-the-oven pizza!

1 loaf French bread
15-oz. can pizza sauce
1 lb. ground pork sausage,
   browned and drained

3-1/2 oz. pkg. sliced pepperoni
8-oz. pkg. shredded mozzarella
   cheese

Cut loaf in half lengthwise. Place both halves on an ungreased baking sheet, cut-side up. Spread with sauce; top with sausage, pepperoni and cheese. Bake at 350 degrees for 15 minutes, or until golden and cheese melts. Slice to serve. Makes 6 to 8 servings.

Herbed Ripe Tomatoes

Out-of-this-world delicious made with fresh garden tomatoes!

4 tomatoes, sliced
2 T. fresh parsley, chopped
1 T. cider vinegar or tarragon
   vinegar
2 T. olive oil

1 T. mustard
1 clove garlic, crushed
1/2 t. salt
1/8 t. pepper

Place tomatoes in a shallow serving dish; set aside. Combine remaining ingredients in a covered jar. Add lid and shake well to mix. Pour mixture over tomatoes. Cover loosely; let stand at room temperature at least 20 minutes before serving. Serves 4 to 6.

Set out all the fixin's for mini pizzas. Let everyone choose their favorite toppers, then pop the pizzas in the oven... a fun family meal or a festive party treat.

LOTSA LASAGNA, PASTA & PIZZA

BBQ Chicken Pizza

Use leftovers to make this pizza! Try it with sliced grilled steak too.

12-inch pre-baked Italian
   pizza crust
3 c. cooked chicken, shredded

1 c. barbecue sauce
1 c. shredded mozzarella cheese
1/2 c. shredded Cheddar cheese

Place pizza crust on a lightly greased 12" pizza pan; set aside. Combine chicken and barbecue sauce in a bowl; spread on pizza crust. Sprinkle with cheeses. Bake at 450 degrees for 8 to 10 minutes, until cheeses melt and crust is crisp. Cut into wedges. Serves 4.

Hot! Buffalo Chicken Pizza

According to Garfield, "It don't mean a thing if it ain't got that zing!" Mmm...pass the napkins!

12-inch pre-baked Italian
   pizza crust
1/4 c. butter, melted
1/4 c. hot cayenne pepper sauce,
   or to taste

2 c. cooked chicken, diced
1/2 c. celery, chopped
4-oz. pkg. crumbled
   blue cheese

Place pizza crust on a lightly greased 12" pizza pan; set aside. Combine butter and sauce in a bowl; mix well. Add chicken and celery; toss to coat. Spread chicken mixture evenly over crust. Sprinkle with cheese. Bake at 450 degrees for 10 to 12 minutes, or until heated through and crust is crisp. Cut into wedges. Serves 6.

Cheesy White Pizza

Deliciously different...even our favorite pizza-loving cat likes a change now & then!

16-oz. pkg. frozen pizza
  dough, thawed
2 cloves garlic, minced
8-oz. pkg. shredded mozzarella
  cheese, divided
1/2 c. grated Parmesan cheese,
  divided

2 roma tomatoes, thinly sliced
seasoned salt to taste
Optional: 4-oz. pkg. pepperoni
  slices

Spread dough on a lightly greased 15" pizza pan. Bake at 425 degrees for 3 to 5 minutes, until dough rises. Spread garlic over crust; sprinkle with half each of the cheeses. Top with tomatoes and seasoned salt; add pepperoni, if desired, and remaining cheeses. Bake at 425 degrees for 8 to 10 minutes, until crisp and golden. Cut into wedges. Makes 8 to 10 servings.

Country Market Marinade Salad

Fresh and zesty! Try other veggies too, like snow peas, carrot coins and radishes.

4 tomatoes, sliced
1 cucumber, peeled and thinly
  sliced
1/2 onion, thinly sliced
3/4 c. canola oil
1/2 c. white vinegar

1 T. fresh basil, chopped
1 T. fresh tarragon, chopped
1 t. salt
1/4 t. pepper
1 head romaine or iceberg
  lettuce, chopped

Arrange tomatoes, cucumber and onion in a shallow serving dish; set aside. In a separate bowl, combine oil, vinegar, herbs and seasonings. Whisk until well blended; pour over vegetables. Cover and refrigerate for 5 to 6 hours. To serve, use a slotted spoon to arrange vegetables over lettuce. Serve with remaining marinade, if desired. Serves 4.

LOTSA LASAGNA, PASTA & PIZZA

Fresh Bruschetta Pizza

With savory twists like this, we could eat pizza seven days a week!

10 roma tomatoes, chopped
1/2 c. red onion, finely chopped
1/4 c. plus 1 T. olive oil, divided
1/4 c. balsamic vinegar
2 T. fresh basil, chopped
6 cloves garlic, minced
1/4 t. garlic salt

1/2 t. pepper
11-oz. tube refrigerated pizza
  crust
1/2 c. pizza sauce
8-oz. pkg. shredded Italian-
  blend cheese
dried oregano to taste

In a large bowl, combine tomatoes, onion, 1/4 cup oil, vinegar, basil, garlic and seasonings. Stir to blend; set aside. Unroll crust and place on a lightly greased baking sheet. Spread with sauce. Drain any excess liquid from tomato mixture; spoon over crust. Sprinkle with cheese and oregano; drizzle with remaining oil. Bake at 400 degrees for 13 to 18 minutes, until crust is crisp and golden. Cut into squares. Serves 6.

Mmm...cheese! Golden cheese crisps are tasty with salads or just as a snack. Spoon mounds of freshly shredded Parmesan cheese, 4 inches apart, onto a baking sheet lined with parchment paper. Bake at 400 degrees for 5 to 7 minutes, until melted and golden, then cool.

Meatball Pizza Pockets

Try adding a cup of chopped mushrooms, diced green peppers or black olives instead of the spinach...you can even mix & match!

14-oz. pkg. frozen meatballs,
  thawed and halved
1-1/2 c. spaghetti sauce
1 c. ricotta cheese
1 c. shredded mozzarella cheese

10-oz. pkg. frozen chopped
  spinach, thawed and drained
13.8-oz. tube refrigerated pizza
  crust

In a bowl, combine meatballs, sauce, cheeses and spinach; set aside. On a lightly greased baking sheet, roll out dough to a 12-inch by 10-inch rectangle. Cut dough into 4 equal pieces. Spoon cheese mixture evenly over each dough piece, leaving a one-inch border. Fold dough over mixture and pinch to seal shut. Arrange pizza pockets on baking sheet, seam-side down. Bake at 425 degrees for 18 to 22 minutes, until golden. Makes 4 servings.

For a quick last-minute pizza party appetizer, drain a jar of Italian antipasto mix and toss with bite-size cubes of mozzarella cheese. Serve with cocktail picks.

Food...it's just another word for

IT'S DINNER TIME...
NOW!!!

Mom's Meatloaf

*Eat till you explode! Jon and Garfield always bring home a
heapin' helpin' of Mom's amazing meatloaf after visiting the farm.*

2 eggs, beaten
3/4 c. saltine crackers, crushed
1/4 c. onion, chopped
1/4 c. green pepper, finely
    chopped
8-oz. can tomato sauce
1 T. Worcestershire sauce

1 t. salt
1/2 t. pepper
1-1/2 lbs. ground beef
1/2 c. catsup
2 t. mustard
2 T. brown sugar, packed

In a large bowl, stir together eggs, cracker crumbs, onion, green pepper,
sauces and seasonings. Add beef; mix well with your hands and form
into a loaf. Place in an ungreased 9"x5" loaf pan. Bake, uncovered, at
350 degrees for one hour. Combine remaining ingredients in a small
bowl. Spread over meatloaf; bake an additional 10 to 15 minutes.
Serves 6.

Buttery Mashed Potatoes

*A "must" with meatloaf! And pot roast, and chicken & noodles,
and turkey & gravy...oh, just pass the potatoes!*

6 to 8 Yukon Gold potatoes,
    peeled and cubed
1/2 c. butter, softened

1 c. evaporated milk
salt and pepper to taste

Cover potatoes with water in a large saucepan; bring to a boil over
medium-high heat. Cook until tender, about 15 minutes; drain. Add
remaining ingredients. Beat with an electric mixer on medium speed
until well blended and creamy. Serves 8 to 10.

For perfect mashed potatoes, warm the milk a little
before adding it to the potatoes.

Super Saucy Meatballs

You haven't tasted meatballs 'til you've eaten these creamy mouthfuls! Serve over noodles or rice for a real tummy-filling meal.

2 lbs. ground beef
1-1/2 c. dry bread crumbs
1-1/2 oz. pkg. onion soup mix
8-oz. container sour cream
1 egg, beaten
1/3 c. all-purpose flour

1 t. paprika
1/4 c. butter
10-3/4 oz. can cream of chicken soup
3/4 c. milk

In a large bowl, combine beef, crumbs, soup mix, sour cream and egg. Mix well; form into walnut-size meatballs. In a shallow dish, combine flour and paprika; roll meatballs in mixture. Melt butter in a large skillet over medium-high heat. Brown meatballs; drain and return to skillet. Blend together soup and milk in a separate bowl; spoon over meatballs. Cover and simmer over low heat for about 20 minutes. Makes 6 to 8 servings.

Cook once, eat twice! Make a double batch of meatloaf, meatballs or taco beef, then freeze half. On a busy night, it's terrific to simply pull a homemade dinner from the freezer, reheat and serve.

IT'S DINNER TIME...
NOW!!!

Best Baked Mac & Cheese

Just like Mom's...boxed mac & cheese can't hold a candle to it!

8-oz. pkg. elbow macaroni,
   uncooked
1 egg, beaten
1 T. hot water
1 t. dry mustard

1 t. salt
1 c. milk
12-oz. pkg. shredded sharp
   Cheddar cheese, divided

Cook macaroni according to package directions; drain and return to cooking pot. In a small bowl, whisk together egg, water, mustard and salt; add to macaroni. Pour in milk and stir well. Add most of cheese, reserving 3/4 cup to sprinkle on top. Pour macaroni mixture into a buttered 2-quart casserole dish. Sprinkle with reserved cheese. Bake, uncovered, at 350 degrees for 35 to 45 minutes, until bubbly and golden. Makes 6 to 8 servings.

Love a crunchy crumb topping on your macaroni & cheese?
Toss some soft fresh bread crumbs with a little melted
butter and sprinkle them on the unbaked casserole. Bake it,
uncovered, until the crumbs are crisp and golden.

Batter-Top Chicken Pot Pie

With this recipe, you can turn Turkey Day leftovers into a delicious dinner too! Just use 3 cups leftover roast turkey, one cup turkey or chicken broth and 2 cups cooked veggies.

3 to 4 lbs. chicken
10-3/4 oz. can cream of
   chicken soup
10-3/4 oz. can cream of
   celery soup
16-oz. pkg. frozen mixed
   vegetables, thawed

garlic powder, salt and pepper
   to taste
1 c. all-purpose flour
1 c. milk
1/2 c. butter, melted

Cover chicken pieces with water in a stockpot. Bring to a boil over medium heat. Reduce heat to medium-low and simmer until chicken is tender, about one hour. Remove chicken to a plate, reserving one cup broth. Shred chicken when cool, discarding skin and bones. In a greased 13"x9" baking pan, mix together chicken, soups, reserved broth, vegetables and seasonings. In a bowl, stir together flour, milk and butter until smooth; spread over chicken mixture. Bake, uncovered, at 350 degrees for 45 minutes to one hour, until bubbly and crust is golden. Makes 6 to 8 servings.

Freeze extra homemade chicken broth in ice cube trays for down-home flavor when cooking rice or pasta. Cubes of frozen broth are handy when whipping up gravies or sauces too.

IT'S DINNER TIME... NOW!!!

Dijon Beef Stew

*Serve this savory stew ladled over split biscuits for
an extra hearty dinner.*

1-1/2 lbs. stew beef cubes
1/4 c. all-purpose flour
2 T. oil
salt and pepper to taste
14-1/2 oz. can beef broth
2 potatoes, peeled and cubed

2 14-1/2 oz. cans diced
   tomatoes with garlic
   and onion
1 c. baby carrots
3/4 t. dried thyme
2 T. Dijon mustard

Combine beef cubes and flour in a large plastic zipping bag; toss to
coat evenly. In a large stockpot, heat oil over medium-high heat. Add
beef and brown on all sides. Season beef with salt and pepper; stir in
remaining ingredients except mustard. Bring to a boil; reduce heat to
low. Cover and simmer, stirring occasionally, for one hour, or until
beef is tender. Gently stir in mustard just before serving. Serves 6 to 8.

Browning adds lots of flavor to beef stew! For the very best
flavor, pat the stew cubes dry with a paper towel before
browning. Don't crowd the pieces in the pan, and be sure
to stir up all the tasty browned bits at the bottom.

Baked Chicken & Noodles

Perfect for Sunday dinner, Garfield-style...with a big nap afterwards!

2-1/2 lbs. boneless, skinless
   chicken breasts, cut into
   large cubes
3 T. butter, melted
1/2 t. lemon zest
1 t. paprika
3/4 t. dried marjoram

1/2 t. pepper
4 c. wide egg noodles, uncooked
1-1/4 c. chicken broth
1 T. cornstarch
1/2 c. grated Parmesan cheese
1 T. dried parsley

Place chicken cubes in a single layer in a lightly greased deep
13"x9" baking pan. In a small bowl, mix together melted butter, zest
and seasonings; spoon mixture over chicken. Bake, uncovered, at
375 degrees for 45 to 50 minutes, until chicken juices run clear when
pierced. While chicken is baking, cook noodles according to package
directions; drain. Remove chicken from baking pan to a bowl; cover
to keep warm. Pour pan drippings into a saucepan over medium heat;
stir in broth and cornstarch. Bring to a boil, stirring constantly, until
mixture is thick and bubbly. Stir in cooked noodles, cheese and
parsley. To serve, spoon chicken over noodle mixture. Serves 4 to 6.

The lazy way to cook egg noodles...bring water to a rolling
boil, then turn off the heat. Add noodles and let stand
for 20 to 30 minutes, stirring twice. It really works!

IT'S DINNER TIME...
NOW!!!

Sour Cream Pork Chop Bake

*If loving pork is wrong, Garfield doesn't want to be right!
Pork chops and potatoes in a creamy sauce...it's a mouthwatering
meal-in-one! Pig out!*

1 T. oil
4 to 6 thick pork chops
salt and pepper to taste
10-3/4 oz. can cream of
    mushroom soup with
    roasted garlic

1/4 c. milk
1 c. sour cream
3 stalks celery, chopped
1/8 t. paprika
4 c. redskin potatoes, sliced
Garnish: dried parsley

Heat oil in a large skillet; add pork chops and brown on both sides.
Season chops with salt and pepper; remove from skillet and set aside.
In a bowl, mix together soup, milk, sour cream, celery and paprika.
Arrange potatoes in a lightly greased 13"x9" baking pan. Spoon soup
mixture over potatoes. Arrange chops over soup, pressing down to
partially cover chops. Sprinkle with parsley. Cover and bake at
375 degrees for 1-1/4 hours, or until chops are very tender.
Makes 4 to 6 servings.

Keep a big shaker jar of seasoned flour by the stove
to sprinkle on pork chops and chicken before frying.
A good mix is one cup flour, 1/4 cup seasoned salt
and one tablespoon pepper.

Delicious Drummies

Bring on the napkins! You're never too old to love eating chicken drumsticks with your hands...or paws!

1/2 c. all-purpose flour	1/4 t. pepper
1/2 t. paprika	1/4 c. butter, melted
1 t. salt	1-1/2 lbs. chicken drumsticks

Mix flour and seasonings in a shallow bowl; place butter in a separate shallow bowl. Dip drumsticks into butter; roll in flour mixture to coat. Arrange in an ungreased 8"x8" baking pan. Bake, uncovered, at 425 degrees for about 50 minutes, until chicken juices run clear when pierced. Makes 4 to 6 servings.

Old-Fashioned Scalloped Potatoes

Add some cubed ham to make this casserole a hearty main dish.

2 T. all-purpose flour	2/3 c. sweet onion, thinly sliced
1 t. salt	2 T. butter, sliced
1/4 t. pepper	1-1/2 c. milk
4 c. potatoes, peeled and thinly sliced	Garnish: paprika

Mix together flour, salt and pepper in a cup; set aside. In a greased 2-quart casserole dish, layer half each of the potatoes, onion, flour mixture and butter. Repeat layers; set aside. Heat milk just to boiling and pour over potatoes; sprinkle with paprika. Bake, covered, at 375 degrees for 45 minutes. Uncover and bake an additional 10 minutes, or until potatoes are tender and golden. Serves 8.

IT'S DINNER TIME...
NOW!!!

Crispy Chicken Nuggets

You'll be crowing about this dish for days! Serve with little cups of your favorite dipping sauce...yummy!

1/2 c. butter, melted
1 c. dry bread crumbs
1/2 c. grated Parmesan cheese
1 t. garlic powder

salt and pepper to taste
3 boneless, skinless chicken
  breasts, cut into strips
  or cubes

Place melted butter in a small bowl. In a separate bowl, mix together bread crumbs, cheese and seasonings. Dip chicken into butter, then into crumb mixture. Place chicken in a single layer on a lightly greased baking sheet. Bake at 400 degrees for 20 minutes, or until chicken juices run clear when pierced. Makes 4 servings.

Spicy Roasted Potatoes

Choose small redskins...no peeling or slicing required. So easy!

1-1/2 to 2 lbs. new redskin
  potatoes
1/4 c. Dijon mustard
2 t. paprika

1 t. chili powder
1 t. ground cumin
1/2 t. cayenne pepper

Pierce potatoes several times with a fork. Place in a large plastic zipping bag; set aside. Blend remaining ingredients in a small bowl; drizzle mixture over potatoes. Seal bag and shake to coat well. Place potatoes in a lightly greased shallow roasting pan. Bake, uncovered, for 35 to 40 minutes, until potatoes are tender. Serves 4 to 6.

Newfangled Tuna Penne Casserole

Shh...don't tell Mom, but this casserole is just as delicious as her good ol' tuna & noodles, and a little bit healthier too!

2-1/4 c. whole-wheat penne
  pasta, uncooked
1/2 lb. sliced mushrooms
2 green onions, minced
1/4 c. fresh Italian parsley,
  minced
1 to 2 6-oz. cans tuna, drained

8-oz. container reduced-fat
  sour cream
1/2 c. light mayonnaise
2 t. Dijon mustard
Optional: 2 T. dry white wine
1/2 c. shredded Cheddar cheese

Cook pasta according to package directions; drain and return to pan.
Meanwhile, spray a skillet with non-stick vegetable spray. Add
mushrooms, onions and parsley. Cook over medium heat until
mushrooms are tender, about 5 minutes. Add tuna; cook until
heated through. Stir tuna mixture into pasta; blend in sour cream,
mayonnaise, mustard and wine, if using. Spread in a lightly greased
2-quart casserole dish. Top with cheese. Bake, uncovered, at
375 degrees for 30 minutes. Serves 2.

Frozen packages of chopped onion, green peppers and
stir-fry vegetables can really speed up mealtime prep...
no chopping, mincing or dicing! It's already done for you.

IT'S DINNER TIME...
NOW!!!

Oven-Fried Catfish

*This crispy fish just calls out for some coleslaw,
so check out our recipe on page 153.*

1 c. yellow cornmeal
1/2 c. all-purpose flour
2 t. salt
2 t. cayenne pepper
4 6-oz. catfish, tilapia or
    haddock fillets, thawed
    if frozen

2 T. oil
Garnish: tartar sauce or
    malt vinegar

Combine dry ingredients; coat fish on both sides with cornmeal mixture. Spread oil over baking sheet; place fish on baking sheet, leaving plenty of room between pieces. Bake at 400 degrees for 20 to 25 minutes. Serve with tartar sauce or vinegar. Serves 4.

Hushpuppies

These golden bites are doggone good with butter or honey.

2 c. yellow cornmeal
1 c. all-purpose flour
14-3/4 oz. can cream-style
    corn
1/4 c. sugar

1 egg, beaten
1 T. baking powder
1 T. onion, minced
salt and pepper to taste
oil for deep frying

In a large bowl, mix all ingredients except oil until smooth. Heat 2 inches of oil to 375 degrees in a saucepan over medium-high heat. Drop batter by tablespoonfuls into hot oil, a few at a time. Fry until golden; drain on paper towels. Serve warm. Makes about 3 dozen.

A Chinese-style bamboo strainer is handy for
gently lifting deep-fried foods from the cooking oil.

Yummy Chicken Quesadillas

Garfield has a mouth with a death wish. If you do too,
turn up the heat with spicy salsa and hot pepper sauce!

3 to 4-lb. deli roast chicken
3 T. salsa
salt and pepper to taste
1 onion, cut into strips
1 green or red pepper,
   cut into strips
3 T. olive oil

15-oz. can refried beans
8 10-inch flour tortillas
3/4 c. shredded Mexican-blend
   cheese
Garnish: shredded lettuce,
   diced tomatoes, sour cream,
   salsa, guacamole

Shred chicken, discarding skin and bones. Place chicken in a bowl. Stir
in salsa, salt and pepper; set aside. In a skillet over medium heat, cook
onion and pepper in oil until crisp-tender; remove to a separate bowl.
Spread refried beans evenly onto 4 tortillas. For each quesadilla, place
one tortilla, bean-side up, in a skillet coated with non-stick vegetable
spray. Top tortilla with 1/4 each of chicken mixture, onion mixture,
cheese and a plain tortilla. Cook over medium heat until layers start to
become warm, about 2 minutes. Carefully turn over; cook until tortilla
is crisp and filling is hot. Cut each quesadilla into wedges and garnish
as desired. Serves 4.

For Taco Night, a muffin tin
makes a super garnish
server. Fill each cup with
something different...salsa,
sour cream, shredded
cheese and diced tomatoes.
So easy to take to the table!

IT'S DINNER TIME...
NOW!!!

Simple & Hearty Burritos

*With just five main ingredients, you'll be chowing down
on these in no time!*

1 lb. ground beef or ground
   pork sausage
15-oz. can chili
16-oz. can refried beans
2 to 4 T. taco seasoning mix

8 10-inch flour tortillas
Garnish: salsa, sour cream,
   shredded cheese, chopped
   tomato, chopped onion,
   shredded lettuce

Brown beef or sausage in a skillet over medium heat; drain. Stir in
chili and beans; add taco seasoning to taste. Simmer until hot and
bubbly. Spoon mixture onto tortillas. Add desired toppings and roll up.
Serves 6 to 8.

Scrumptious Mexican Salad

*Whip up this colorful salad ahead of time...that's one less dish
to get ready at dinnertime!*

2 c. fresh or frozen corn,
   cooked
1 pt. cherry tomatoes, halved

1 avocado, halved, pitted
   and cubed
1/2 c. red onion, finely diced

Combine all ingredients in a large salad bowl. Drizzle with Lime
Dressing; toss gently to mix. Cover and chill until serving time.
Serves 6.

Lime Dressing:

2 T. olive oil
1 T. lime juice
1/2 t. lime zest

1/4 c. fresh cilantro, chopped
1/2 t. salt
1/2 t. pepper

Whisk together ingredients in a small bowl.

Chicken Chimies

The best things in life are edible! Another delicious way
to enjoy a savory rotisserie chicken.

2 to 3 T. oil, divided
2 boneless, skinless chicken
    breasts, cooked and
    shredded
garlic powder, salt and pepper
    to taste

10 8-inch flour tortillas
8-oz. pkg. shredded Monterey
    Jack cheese
1/4 c. green onions, diced
Garnish: sour cream, guacamole

Heat one tablespoon oil in a large skillet over medium heat; add
chicken. Cook and stir for about 3 minutes, until chicken is warmed
through. Add seasonings to taste. Spoon chicken evenly onto tortillas.
Top with cheese and green onions; roll up. Heat remaining oil in a
large skillet over medium-high heat. Add rolled-up tortillas; cook until
golden on all sides. Serve chimies with sour cream and guacamole.
Serves 6 to 8.

A speedy side that goes with any south-of-the-border meal!
Stir some salsa and shredded cheese into hot cooked rice.
Cover and let stand a few minutes until the cheese melts.

IT'S DINNER TIME...
NOW!!!

Spicy Salsa Twists

Just the thing for nights when you're feeling spicy,
but not in the mood for dinner in a tortilla!

8-oz. pkg. rotini pasta,
   uncooked
1 lb. ground beef, browned
   and drained
10-3/4 oz. can tomato soup
1 c. salsa

1/2 c. milk
1 c. shredded Cheddar cheese,
   divided
Garnish: sour cream, barbecue-
   flavored corn chips

Cook pasta according to package directions; drain. Meanwhile, brown
beef in a large skillet over medium heat; drain. Add soup, salsa, milk,
1/2 cup cheese and cooked rotini to beef in skillet. Cook over low heat
until heated through and cheese is melted. Top with remaining cheese.
Serve with sour cream and corn chips. Serves 5.

Simple! Use a potato masher to break up ground beef
quickly and evenly as it browns.

BBQ Pork Ribs

Got a hankering for barbecued ribs on a rainy day? Just pop the tender ribs onto a broiler pan, brush with sauce and broil until done.

12 c. water
4 lbs. pork ribs, cut into
   serving-size portions

1 onion, quartered
2 t. salt
1/4 t. pepper

Pour water into a large stockpot. Bring to a boil over medium-high heat. Add remaining ingredients. Reduce heat to low; cover and simmer for one hour, or until ribs are very tender. Prepare BBQ Sauce while ribs are simmering. Drain ribs and place on a grill over medium-high heat. Grill ribs for 10 minutes on each side, brushing frequently with BBQ Sauce. Serves 4 to 6.

BBQ Sauce:

1/2 c. chili sauce
1/2 c. cider vinegar
1/2 c. brown sugar, packed
1/4 c. Worcestershire sauce
2 T. onion, chopped

1 T. lemon juice
1/2 t. dry mustard
1/8 t. garlic powder
1/8 t. cayenne pepper

Combine all ingredients in a small saucepan. Simmer over low heat, uncovered, for one hour, stirring occasionally.

Take dinner out to the back porch. Use old-fashioned pie tins as plates...serve up bottles of icy root beer and red pop from an ice-filled bucket. Just about anything tastes even better outdoors!

IT'S DINNER TIME...
NOW!!!

Smoky Grilled Corn

The tenderest sweet corn is just-picked, so serve corn on the cob the same day you buy it, whenever possible.

8 ears sweet corn, husks
   removed
1/4 c. olive oil, divided

1 T. kosher salt, divided
1 T. pepper, divided
1 T. smoked paprika, divided

Divide corn between 2 large plastic zipping bags; set aside. Stir together oil and seasonings in a small bowl; drizzle half of mixture into each bag. Close bags and gently toss to coat corn. Remove corn from bags. Place corn on a grill over medium-high heat. Grill corn, turning often, until lightly golden, about 25 minutes. Serves 8.

Farm-Fresh Coleslaw

Take the Garfield lazy way out: buy bagged coleslaw mix and let someone else do the shredding!

3 c. cabbage, shredded
1 c. carrot, peeled and shredded
1/2 c. whipping cream

3 T. cider vinegar
salt and pepper to taste

In a large bowl, combine cabbage and carrot. In a separate small bowl, mix together remaining ingredients. Pour over cabbage mixture and toss to coat. Cover and chill before serving. Makes 6 to 8 servings.

Stop pesky ants from crashing your picnic! Sprinkle salt, crushed chalk or talcum powder in a line around the picnic table...they won't cross that line.

I'M MAKING A LITTLE SANDWICH

Ways to make veggies taste yummy

Hide them with lots of cheese and sour cream.
(We don't recommend this!)

Steam veggies to keep the fresh-picked taste. Bring 1/2 inch of water to a boil in a saucepan and add cut-up veggies. Cover and cook for 3 to 5 minutes, until crisp-tender, and toss with a little butter.

Drop a chicken bouillon cube into the cooking water for extra flavor.

Drizzle steamed veggies with a little olive oil or balsamic vinegar.

Play hide-the-veggies! Keep cooked, chopped veggies in the fridge and toss 'em into your favorite scrambled eggs, noodle dishes, spaghetti sauce, chili or even homemade pizza.

If you don't like a veggie, try eating it fixed a different way. Hate cooked carrots? Try 'em raw and crunchy. Can't stand boiled spinach? Sauté it with a little garlic, salt & pepper. Not keen on sweet potatoes? Mix 'em into regular mashed potatoes. Give peas a chance!

Eating

Marinated Flank Steak

Overnight marinating gives flank steak
mouthwatering flavor.

1-1/2 lbs. beef flank steak,
   cut into 4 pieces
1/2 c. soy sauce
1/4 c. red wine or beef broth
2 T. Worcestershire sauce
2 T. oil

juice of one lime
1/2 bunch green onions,
   chopped
1 clove garlic, minced
1 t. dill weed
1 t. celery seed

Place steak in a large plastic zipping bag; set aside. Combine remaining ingredients; drizzle over steak. Seal bag and refrigerate overnight, turning bag occasionally to coat well. Drain, discarding marinade. Grill steak over medium heat to preferred doneness, 5 to 6 minutes per side for medium-rare. Remove steak to a platter; let stand for 10 minutes. Slice steak on the diagonal with a serrated knife. Serves 4.

Grill some veggies alongside the meat! Brush olive oil over sliced squash, potatoes, peppers or eggplant and grill until tender and golden. You may be surprised how sweet and delicious they are.

IT'S DINNER TIME... NOW!!!

Country-Style Potato Salad

It wouldn't be a picnic without a big bowl of potato salad!

6 to 8 redskin potatoes, cubed
2 t. Dijon mustard
2 t. white wine vinegar
1 t. dried oregano

2 T. oil
4 to 6 green onions, sliced
salt and pepper to taste

Place potatoes in a saucepan; add water to cover. Cook over medium-high heat until tender, about 15 minutes. Drain; place potatoes in a serving bowl. In a separate bowl, whisk together remaining ingredients; pour over potatoes. Toss well; cover and chill before serving. Serves 6 to 8.

Lemony Roasted Broccoli

This dish gives broccoli a good name...and good taste!

1 bunch broccoli, cut into spears
1 T. olive oil
1/4 t. salt

1/4 t. pepper
Garnish: lemon juice

In a bowl, toss broccoli with oil, salt and pepper. Spread on an ungreased baking sheet. Bake at 450 degrees until broccoli is tender and golden, 10 to 12 minutes. Sprinkle with lemon juice and serve. Makes 4 servings.

Zucchini, carrots and other veggies are more fun
to eat when they're cut with a crinkle cutter.
You can turn potatoes into crispy crinkle fries too!

Herbed Grilled Chicken

Chop up leftover grilled chicken and salad veggies to
stuff a pita for lunch tomorrow...yummy!

4 to 6 boneless, skinless
   chicken breasts
1 t. salt
1 t. pepper

3 to 4 T. Dijon mustard
2 T. fresh rosemary, minced
2 T. fresh thyme, minced
2 T. fresh parsley, minced

Season chicken with salt and pepper. Place on a grill over medium heat. Cook for 5 to 6 minutes on each side, until golden and juices run clear. Remove chicken from heat. Brush mustard over both sides; sprinkle with herbs. Serves 4 to 6.

SO MANY MEALS, SO LITTLE TIME

Flattened boneless chicken breasts cook up quickly and evenly. Simply place chicken between two pieces of plastic wrap and gently pound to desired thickness with a meat mallet or a small skillet.

IT'S DINNER TIME...
NOW!!!

Salad on a Stick

A salad you can eat with your hands? Now you're talking!
Besides, everything tastes better on a stick!

8 new redskin potatoes
8 pearl onions
1 green pepper, cut into
    1-inch squares
1 red or yellow pepper, cut into
    1-inch squares

16 cherry tomatoes
1 zucchini, sliced 1/4-inch thick
8 long wooden skewers
Optional: grated Parmesan
    cheese

Cover potatoes with water in a saucepan; bring to a boil over medium heat. Cook for 5 to 8 minutes. Add onions to saucepan; continue cooking for 5 minutes, or until potatoes and onions are tender. Drain and cool. Thread all vegetables alternately onto skewers. Arrange skewers in a large shallow dish; drizzle with Red Wine Vinaigrette. Cover and refrigerate at least one hour, turning frequently. At serving time, sprinkle with cheese, if desired. Makes 8 servings.

Red Wine Vinaigrette:

2/3 c. olive oil
1/3 c. red wine vinegar
2 cloves garlic, minced

1 T. dried oregano
1 t. salt
1/4 t. pepper

Whisk together all ingredients.

Souvenir tea towels make fun-to-use oversized napkins... perfect when enjoying messy-but-tasty foods like barbecued ribs, buttered corn on the cob and juicy wedges of watermelon!

Sunday Chicken & Vegetables

Mmm...juicy roast chicken with crisp golden skin! Once you've learned how, it's just as easy to roast two chickens at once. Refrigerate the second chicken to use in lots of other recipes.

3 to 3-1/2 lb. roasting chicken
1 T. plus 1 t. olive oil, divided
1 t. dried thyme
1/2 t. salt
1/2 t. pepper
4 potatoes, peeled and cubed

6 carrots, peeled and cut into
   2-inch pieces
6 stalks celery, cut into
   2-inch pieces
1 to 2 onions, cut into wedges

Place chicken in an ungreased roasting pan. Tie the legs together with kitchen string, if desired. Brush one teaspoon oil over chicken; sprinkle with seasonings. Bake, uncovered, at 475 degrees for 15 minutes. Toss vegetables with remaining oil; add to pan around chicken. Reduce oven to 400 degrees. Bake for an additional 35 to 45 minutes, until juices run clear when the thickest part of thigh is pierced. Remove chicken to a serving platter; cover loosely with aluminum foil. Let stand for 10 to 15 minutes before slicing. Serves 6.

Don't throw away roast chicken bones...use them to make flavorful chicken broth! Cover bones with water in a stockpot. Onion, carrot and celery trimmings can be added too. Simmer gently for 30 to 40 minutes, then strain in a colander. Refrigerate or freeze broth in recipe-size containers.

IT'S DINNER TIME...
NOW!!!

Mom's Very Best Stuffing

*Whether you call it stuffing or dressing, the best is made
from day-old bread. If your loaf is really fresh, let the pieces
dry on a baking sheet for a couple of hours first.*

1 loaf white bread, torn into
   bite-size pieces
1/2 c. butter, melted and
   slightly cooled
2 eggs, beaten

1 onion, finely chopped
1 stalk celery, finely chopped
1-1/4 t. dried sage
1 c. chicken broth

Place bread in a large bowl; pour butter and eggs over bread and toss
to mix. Add onion, celery and sage; toss gently. Add just enough broth
to moisten bread to desired consistency. Spoon mixture into a buttered
1-1/2 quart casserole dish. Bake, covered, at 325 degrees for 45 to 50
minutes. Uncover during the last 10 to 15 minutes if a drier texture is
preferred. Serves 6.

Whip up some pan gravy...it's simple! Place the roast on a
platter. Set the roasting pan with pan juices on the stovetop
over medium heat. Shake together 1/4 cup cold water and
1/4 cup cornstarch in a small jar and pour into the pan. Cook
and stir until gravy comes to a boil and thickens, 5 to
10 minutes. Season to taste with salt and pepper.

Incredibly Easy Pot Roast

Yum...this roast even makes its own savory gravy!

3 to 4-lb. boneless beef chuck
   roast
10-3/4 oz. can cream of
   mushroom soup
1-1/2 oz. pkg. onion soup mix

2 to 3 potatoes, peeled and
   quartered
8 to 10 baby carrots
1 onion, cut into wedges

Place roast on a long piece of aluminum foil. Spoon soup over roast;
sprinkle with soup mix. Arrange vegetables on top. Bring the edges of
the foil together and seal well. Place package in a roasting pan. Bake
at 350 degrees for 2-1/2 to 3 hours, without peeking, until roast is
tender. Let stand for 10 minutes before serving; open foil carefully
(steam will be hot). Serves 6 to 8.

To make in a slow cooker:

Place vegetables in a large slow cooker. Place roast on top (do not
wrap in foil). Top with soup and soup mix. Cover and cook on low
setting for 9 to 10 hours, until roast is tender.

Food for friends doesn't
have to be fancy...your
guests will be thrilled with
old-fashioned comfort
foods. Let everyone help
themselves from big
platters set right on the
table...they'll love it!

IT'S DINNER TIME...
NOW!!!

Creamy Potatoes & Baby Peas

If the potatoes are very small, you don't need to cube them.

2-1/2 c. new redskin potatoes,
   cubed
1/2 c. fresh or frozen baby peas
2 T. butter, softened

2 c. milk, divided
2 T. all-purpose flour
salt and pepper to taste

Place potatoes in a large saucepan; cover with water. Cook over medium-high heat until potatoes are tender, about 15 minutes; add peas during last 4 minutes. Drain; return to saucepan and add butter. In a small bowl, whisk together 1/4 cup milk and flour until thickened; set aside. Pour remaining milk over potatoes and peas; heat through. Stir in flour mixture; continue cooking until thickened and warmed through. Season with salt and pepper before serving. Serves 4.

Mustard-Glazed Carrots

Don't say you don't like carrots until you try these babies!

16-oz. pkg. baby carrots
1/2 t. salt
1-1/2 T. butter, softened

1-1/2 T. yellow or Dijon mustard
1/4 c. brown sugar, packed
2 T. fresh parsley, chopped

Slice carrots in half lengthwise; place in a saucepan. Cover carrots with water; add salt. Cover and simmer over medium-high heat for about 20 minutes, until tender. Drain and return to saucepan. In a separate small saucepan, mix butter, mustard and brown sugar. Cook and stir over medium heat for 3 minutes, or until syrupy. Drizzle butter mixture over carrots; simmer for 5 minutes. Sprinkle with parsley before serving. Makes 6 servings.

Brown Sugar-Glazed Baked Ham

A very special meal to share...and just think of all the delicious ham sandwiches you can make with the leftovers!

8 to 10-lb. fully-cooked
    bone-in ham
1-1/2 c. water
1-1/4 c. brown sugar, packed
1/3 c. pineapple juice

1/3 c. honey
2 T. Dijon mustard
1 T. orange juice
2 t. orange zest
1/4 t. ground cloves

Place ham in an ungreased roasting pan; pour water into pan. Set aside while making glaze. In a saucepan over medium heat, whisk together remaining ingredients. Bring to a boil; reduce heat to low and simmer for 5 to 10 minutes. Brush glaze over ham; tent loosely with aluminum foil. Bake at 325 degrees for 2 hours. Remove foil; brush glaze over ham. Bake, uncovered, for an additional 30 minutes, brushing with glaze every 10 minutes. Place ham on a serving platter; cover loosely with foil. Let stand for 15 to 20 minutes before slicing. Makes 10 to 15 servings.

Baked sweet potatoes are yummy with baked ham. Pierce potatoes several times with a fork, and put them right on the oven rack. At 325 degrees, they'll be tender in about one hour. Top with butter and sprinkle with cinnamon-sugar. It couldn't be easier!

IT'S DINNER TIME...
NOW!!!

Minty Cool Green Bean Salad

A scrumptious new way to enjoy garden-fresh green beans.
Spoon the salad into canning jars to tuck in a picnic cooler.

1-1/2 lbs. green beans, trimmed
    and cut into bite-size pieces
1 t. garlic, minced
1/2 t. salt
1/4 c. white wine vinegar
2 T. lemon juice

salt and pepper to taste
1/4 c. olive oil
2 T. fresh mint, minced
1 T. fresh basil, minced
1/2 c. red onion, minced

Bring a large saucepan of water to a boil over high heat. Add beans
and cook for 3 to 5 minutes, until crisp-tender; drain. Transfer beans
to a bowl of ice water to chill; drain well. Combine garlic and salt in a
small bowl; crush to a paste consistency with the back of a spoon. Add
vinegar, lemon juice, salt and pepper; whisk to blend. Add oil and
herbs; whisk until well blended. In a serving bowl, combine beans and
onion. Add dressing and toss to coat. Chill 20 minutes before serving.
Makes 4 servings.

It's a snap to steam vegetables in the microwave. Place sliced
veggies in a microwave-safe dish and add a little water. Cover
with plastic wrap and vent with a knife tip. Microwave on high
for 2 to 5 minutes, checking after each minute, until crisp-
tender. Uncover carefully to let hot steam escape.

Baked Turkey Drumstick

*Treat yourself on a lazy day! Or double the recipe
and share with a friend.*

1 turkey drumstick
2 slices bacon, crisply cooked
   and crumbled
2 T. bacon drippings or olive oil

2 T. onion, chopped
2 T. celery, chopped
1/8 t. celery salt
salt and pepper to taste

Place drumstick in the center of a piece of aluminum foil. Top with remaining ingredients. Wrap foil tightly around drumstick; place in a shallow baking pan. Bake at 400 degrees for 1-1/2 hours, or until juices run clear when drumstick is pierced. Makes one serving.

Garlicky Parmesan Asparagus

Roasted asparagus is tasty too. Toss the butter, oil, garlic and asparagus together. Spread on a baking sheet and bake at 425 degrees for 10 to 15 minutes. Sprinkle with remaining ingredients.

1 T. butter, melted
2 T. olive oil
2 cloves garlic, minced
1 lb. asparagus spears, trimmed
   and cut into bite-size pieces

2 t. lemon juice
salt and pepper to taste
Garnish: shredded Parmesan
   cheese

In a skillet over medium heat, combine butter, oil and garlic; cook and stir for one to 2 minutes. Add asparagus. Cook to desired tenderness, stirring occasionally, about 10 minutes. Drain; sprinkle asparagus with remaining ingredients. Makes 4 servings.

IT'S DINNER TIME...
NOW!!!

Hot Bacon Brussels Sprouts

Bacon to the rescue...now even Garfield
might eat Brussels sprouts!

1-1/2 lbs. Brussels sprouts,
   trimmed and quartered
1 T. olive oil
1/2 t. salt

5 slices bacon
1/4 c. balsamic vinegar
1 T. brown sugar, packed
1/2 t. Dijon mustard

In a large bowl, toss Brussels sprouts with oil and salt. Line a rimmed
baking sheet with aluminum foil; add sprouts in a single layer. Bake,
uncovered, at 400 degrees for 20 minutes, or until tender and golden.
Meanwhile, in a skillet over medium heat, cook bacon until crisp.
Remove bacon to a paper towel-lined plate; drain. Reserve
2 tablespoons drippings in skillet. Add remaining ingredients to skillet.
Cook over medium-high heat, stirring frequently, for 4 to 6 minutes,
until liquid cooks down by half. Drizzle over sprouts, tossing gently to
coat. Sprinkle with crumbled bacon. Serves 4 to 6.

GARFIELD, SEE WHAT
THIS TASTES LIKE

Bacon drippings may be poured into a jar and kept in
the fridge. Add a spoonful or two when cooking
hashbrown potatoes, green beans or pan gravy
for wonderful down-home flavor.

Tossed Salad with Sherry Dressing

*This salad is delicious, and the ingredients can be found any
time of year. Try it with a pear in place of the apple too.*

1 bunch romaine, red leaf or
   green leaf lettuce, torn
1 apple, cored and chopped
1/4 c. red onion, chopped

1/4 c. sweetened dried
   cranberries
1/4 c. sliced almonds
1/4 c. crumbled blue cheese

Toss together lettuce, apple and onion in a large salad bowl. Drizzle
with desired amount of Sherry Dressing; toss to coat. Top with
remaining ingredients. Serves 4.

Sherry Dressing:

3/4 c. olive oil
3 T. sherry wine vinegar

3 T. lemon juice
1 T. Dijon mustard

Whisk together all ingredients; pour into a covered jar. Keep
refrigerated; shake before using.

Make a frosty pitcher of
strawberry lemonade! In a tall
pitcher, combine a 12-ounce can
of frozen lemonade concentrate,
a 10-ounce package of frozen
strawberries and 4-1/2 cups of
cold water. Let stand until berries
thaw, then stir well. Wonderful!

It wouldn't be a party without DESSERT!

Golden Birthday Cake

When his birthday rolls around on June 19, Garfield likes to get cake-faced! Decorate this one with pink frosting and lots of candy sprinkles.

4 eggs, separated
1 c. butter, softened
2 c. sugar
2 t. vanilla extract
3 c. all-purpose flour

1-1/2 t. baking powder
1/2 t. salt
1 c. milk
Garnish: favorite frosting

With an electric mixer on high speed, beat egg whites in a bowl until stiff peaks form; set aside. In a separate large bowl, beat butter on medium speed; gradually beat in sugar until fluffy. Beat in egg yolks and vanilla. Combine flour, baking powder and salt in another bowl; stir into butter mixture alternately with milk. Fold in egg whites. Divide batter among 3 greased and floured 9" round cake pans. Bake at 350 degrees for 35 minutes, until a toothpick inserted in the center tests clean. Turn out layers onto a wire rack; cool completely. Assemble cake with frosting. Serves 12.

Best-Ever Bakery Frosting

Perfect for all kinds of cakes and cookies!

2 16-oz. pkgs. powdered sugar
1 c. shortening

1 t. clear vanilla extract
1/2 to 3/4 c. milk

In a large bowl, blend together all ingredients just until moistened, adding milk as needed. Do not overbeat. Makes about 3 cups, enough for a 2-layer cake or 6 dozen cookies.

Mocha Party Cake

Coffee & chocolate...a harmonious combo of two of Garfield's favorites! This delectable, easy-to-make dessert will feed a crowd.

2 c. all-purpose flour
2 c. sugar
1 c. brewed coffee
1/2 c. butter
1/2 c. shortening
1/4 c. baking cocoa

1 t. baking soda
1 t. cinnamon
1 t. vanilla extract
1/2 c. buttermilk
2 eggs, beaten
1/2 c. chopped pecans

Combine flour and sugar in a large bowl; set aside. In a saucepan over medium heat, combine coffee, butter, shortening and cocoa. Bring to a boil; remove from heat. Slowly stir coffee mixture into flour mixture. Add remaining ingredients except pecans; mix well. Pour batter into a greased and floured 13"x9" baking pan. Bake at 400 degrees for 25 minutes, or until center tests done with a toothpick. Remove from oven; immediately spoon Hot Cocoa Frosting over cake. Sprinkle with pecans. Serves 15 to 20.

Hot Cocoa Frosting:

1/2 c. butter
1/4 c. baking cocoa
6 T. milk

16-oz. pkg. powdered sugar
1 t. vanilla extract

In a saucepan over medium heat, combine butter, cocoa and milk; bring to a boil. Add powdered sugar and vanilla. Stir until smooth.

Make sure your sheet cake stays party-perfect. Insert toothpicks halfway into the cake before covering in plastic wrap. They'll keep the plastic wrap from touching the frosting.

Picnic Basket Cake

Fruit, nuts and chocolate...yum! Wrap squares in wax paper to tuck in a lunchbox.

2-1/4 c. all-purpose flour
1 c. brown sugar, packed
2 t. baking soda
1 t. salt
2 eggs, beaten

1/4 c. butter, softened
16-oz. can fruit cocktail
1/2 c. chopped walnuts
1/2 c. semi-sweet chocolate
  chips

In a large bowl, mix flour, brown sugar, baking soda and salt. Add eggs, butter and undrained fruit cocktail. Beat with an electric mixer on medium speed for 2 minutes. Pour batter into a greased and floured 13"x9" baking pan. Sprinkle walnuts and chips on top. Bake at 350 degrees for 35 to 40 minutes, until the center springs back when touched. Let cool before slicing. Makes 12 to 15 servings.

Grease and flour cake pans in a jiffy! Grease the pan, sprinkle with flour, cover with plastic wrap and give it a good shake.

Fudgy Layer Cake

Rich, chocolatey flavor...a fudgy treat that can't be beat!

1/4 c. butter
1/4 c. shortening
2 c. sugar
2 t. vanilla extract
2 eggs, beaten
1-3/4 c. all-purpose flour

3/4 c. baking cocoa
1-1/2 t. baking powder
1-1/2 t. baking soda
3/4 t. salt
1-3/4 c. milk

In a large bowl, blend butter, shortening, sugar and vanilla until fluffy; stir in eggs. In a separate bowl, mix together flour, cocoa, baking powder, baking soda and salt; add to butter mixture alternately with milk. Beat with an electric mixer on medium speed for 2 minutes. Pour batter into 2 greased and floured 9" round cake pans. Bake at 350 degrees for 30 to 35 minutes, until center tests clean with a toothpick. Turn out layers onto a wire rack; cool completely. Assemble cake with Cocoa Frosting. Serves 12.

Cocoa Frosting:

6 T. butter, softened
1/2 c. baking cocoa
2-2/3 c. powdered sugar

2/3 c. milk, divided
1 t. vanilla extract

Stir together butter and cocoa in a large bowl. Add powdered sugar alternately with 1/3 cup milk. Beat until smooth and creamy; add remaining milk to desired consistency. Stir in vanilla.

No more frosting smudges on the cake plate! Tuck strips of wax paper under the edges of the bottom layer. Discard the paper when you're done.

DINNER IS OVER... WHAT'S FOR DESSERT?

Classic Carrot Layer Cake

Delicious to eat and almost good for you!

4 eggs, beaten
1-3/4 c. sugar
1 c. oil
2 c. all-purpose flour
2 t. baking soda
1 t. salt

1 t. cinnamon
1 c. carrot, peeled and shredded
1 c. apple, peeled, cored and
   coarsely chopped
1/2 c. chopped walnuts

In a large bowl, beat together eggs, sugar and oil; set aside. In a
separate bowl, mix together flour, baking soda, salt and cinnamon; stir
into egg mixture. Add carrot, apple and walnuts; mix well. Pour batter
into 2 greased and floured 9" round cake pans. Bake at 350 degrees for
30 to 35 minutes, until a toothpick inserted in the center tests clean.
Set pans on wire racks to cool for 10 minutes. Turn layers out of pans;
cool completely. Assemble cake with Cream Cheese Frosting. Makes
12 servings.

Cream Cheese Frosting:

8-oz. pkg. cream cheese,
   softened
1/2 c. butter, softened

2 t. vanilla extract
4-1/2 to 5 c. powdered sugar

Blend together cream cheese, butter and vanilla until fluffy. Gradually
mix in powdered sugar until smooth.

Vegetables are a must on a diet. I suggest carrot cake,
zucchini bread and pumpkin pie.
–Garfield

Strawberry Shortcake

Nothing says "summertime" like strawberry shortcake! Use juicy ripe peaches for a different take on this wonderful summer treat.

1 c. all-purpose flour
1 t. baking powder
1/2 c. sugar
1 egg, beaten
1/2 c. milk

1-1/4 t. vanilla extract
2 T. butter, softened
3 to 4 c. strawberries, hulled,
   sliced and divided
Garnish: whipped cream

In a large bowl, mix together flour, baking powder and sugar. Add egg, milk and vanilla; stir well. Pour batter into a greased and floured 9" round cake pan. Bake at 350 degrees for 15 to 20 minutes, until set and golden. Turn cake out onto a wire rack; cool slightly. Split cake in half horizontally and place bottom layer on a serving plate. Top with butter and strawberries, reserving a few berries for garnish. Add top layer. Garnish with whipped cream and reserved strawberries. Cut into wedges to serve. Serves 8.

Use a plastic drinking straw to hull strawberries with ease.
Just push the straw through the end without a stem
and the green, leafy top will pop right off!

DINNER IS OVER... WHAT'S FOR DESSERT?

Luscious Strawberry Pie

This pie crust is super-easy to make...no rolling pin needed! But it's fine to use a ready-made pie crust instead. Pie to die for!

1-1/2 c. water
3/4 c. sugar
2 T. cornstarch
1/8 t. salt
3-oz. pkg. strawberry gelatin
   mix

4 c. strawberries, hulled and
   sliced
Garnish: whipped cream

Make and bake Pat & Go Pie Crust; set aside. Meanwhile, in a 2-quart saucepan over medium-high heat, stir together water, sugar, cornstarch and salt. Bring to a boil, stirring until clear; stir in dry gelatin mix until dissolved. Remove from heat; pour 1/4 of gelatin mixture into crust. Arrange strawberries in crust; pour remaining gelatin mixture over the top. Cover and refrigerate until set, 2 to 3 hours. Serve with whipped cream. Serves 8.

Pat & Go Pie Crust:

1 c. all-purpose flour
2 T. powdered sugar

1/2 c. butter, softened

Combine flour and powdered sugar; cut butter into flour mixture with a fork until crumbly. Pat into a 9" pie plate. Bake at 350 degrees for 15 minutes; cool.

To keep berries at their freshest, place unwashed berries in a bowl, cover loosely and place in the coldest part of the fridge for up to 3 days. Gently wash them only when you're ready to use them.

Fresh Peach Pie

*So simple to make...simply irresistible to eat. A full belly
is a happy belly!*

2 9-inch pie crusts
10 to 12 peaches, peeled, pitted,
   sliced and divided
1/4 c. butter

1/3 c. all-purpose flour
1 c. plus 1 T. sugar, divided
Garnish: vanilla ice cream

Place one crust in a 9" pie plate. Arrange 1/4 of peach slices in crust. In
a bowl, mix butter, flour and one cup sugar with a fork until crumbly.
Sprinkle 1/4 of butter mixture over peaches. Repeat layers. Add
remaining crust; flute edges and cut vents with a knife tip. Sprinkle
remaining sugar over crust. Bake at 350 degrees for 45 minutes, or
until bubbly and crust is golden. Serve warm, topped with a scoop of
ice cream. Makes 8 servings.

A neighborhood pie party is a tasty way to get together with
nearby friends! Invite everyone to bring their best-loved
pies...you provide the ice cream, whipped cream, beverages
and a big stack of napkins. Easy and fun!

DINNER IS OVER...
WHAT'S FOR DESSERT?

Just Peachy Blueberry Crisp

This summery dessert practically makes itself...it's hard to mess up! Enjoy it year 'round by using frozen peaches and blueberries, but let them thaw first.

3 c. peaches, peeled, pitted
   and sliced
1/2 c. blueberries
2 t. cinnamon-sugar
1 c. all-purpose flour

1 c. brown sugar, packed
1/2 c. butter, softened
3/4 c. long-cooking oats,
   uncooked

Arrange peaches and blueberries in a buttered 8"x8" baking pan. Sprinkle with cinnamon-sugar; toss gently to coat. In a bowl, combine flour and brown sugar; cut in butter and oats with a fork until mixture is crumbly. Sprinkle mixture evenly over fruit. Bake at 350 degrees for 40 to 45 minutes, until topping is crisp and golden. Serve warm. Serves 6 to 8.

Ovens can vary, so set a kitchen timer when the pan goes into the oven. Check for doneness after the shortest baking time given...if a little more time is needed, be sure to watch carefully.

No-Bake Lemon Icebox Pie

Creamy and refreshing! Dress it up with twists of lemon peel.

1-1/2 c. vanilla wafers, finely
  crushed
1/4 to 1/2 c. butter, melted
14-oz. can sweetened condensed
  milk

1/2 c. lemon juice
Optional: several drops yellow
  food coloring
1 c. whipping cream

Stir together vanilla wafer crumbs and butter. Press firmly into an ungreased 9" pie plate; chill for 15 to 20 minutes. In a bowl, stir together condensed milk, lemon juice and food coloring, if using. In a deep bowl, whip cream with an electric mixer on high speed until soft peaks form. Fold whipped cream into condensed milk mixture; spoon into chilled crust. Cover and chill for 3 hours, or until set. Makes 6 to 8 servings.

Turn No-Bake Lemon Icebox Pie into a Margarita Pie!
Use crushed pretzels instead of vanilla wafers for the crust,
adding 1/4 cup sugar to the crumb mixture. In the filling,
use lime juice instead of lemon juice with a bit of
green food coloring.

DINNER IS OVER...
WHAT'S FOR DESSERT?

No-Bake Banana Cream Pie

This old-fashioned dessert never fails to delight.
Soft ripe bananas are perfect.

1 c. milk
3.4-oz. pkg. instant vanilla
   pudding mix
1/2 t. vanilla extract

12-oz. container frozen whipped
   topping, thawed and divided
9-inch graham cracker crust
4 bananas, sliced

Combine milk and dry pudding mix in a large bowl. Beat with an electric mixer on low speed for 2 minutes; beat in vanilla. Use a spoon to fold in 3 cups whipped topping. Spread one cup of pudding mixture in crust; layer with half of bananas. Repeat layers, ending with remaining pudding. Spread with remaining whipped topping. Cover and chill for 2 hours. Makes 8 servings.

Make a good thing even better...sprinkle your No-Bake Banana Cream Pie with toasted coconut. Spread shredded coconut on an ungreased baking sheet. Bake at 350 degrees for 7 to 12 minutes, stirring frequently, until toasted and golden.

Walnut Crunch Pumpkin Pie

A pie you can be thankful for on Thanksgiving!

9-inch pie crust
15-oz. can pumpkin
12-oz. can evaporated milk
2 eggs, beaten
3/4 c. brown sugar, packed

1/2 t. salt
1-1/2 t. cinnamon
1/2 t. nutmeg
1/2 t. ground ginger
Garnish: whipped cream

Place pie crust in a 9" pie plate; set aside. In a large bowl, combine remaining ingredients except garnish. Beat with an electric mixer on medium speed for one minute. Set pie plate on oven rack; pour in pumpkin mixture. Bake at 400 degrees for 40 minutes, or until a knife tip inserted one inch from the edge tests clean. Remove pie from oven; sprinkle evenly with Walnut Topping. Turn oven to broil; place pie about 6 inches below broiler. Broil for 3 minutes, or until topping is golden and sugar is melted. Cool pie on a wire rack. Garnish with whipped cream. Makes 8 to 10 servings.

Walnut Topping:

1 c. chopped walnuts
3/4 c. brown sugar, packed

1/4 c. butter, melted

Mix ingredients well in a small bowl.

Need to chop nuts in a hurry?
Place them in a plastic
zipping bag and roll with a
rolling pin or even a
heavy food can...so easy!

DINNER IS OVER... WHAT'S FOR DESSERT?

Sour Cream Apple Pie

With its buttery, sugary crumb topping, this delectable dessert is easy as pie to make...hard to resist!

9-inch pie crust
2 c. Rome apples, peeled, cored and diced
1/2 c. sugar
2 T. all-purpose flour

1/4 t. salt
8-oz. container sour cream
1 egg, beaten
1-1/2 t. vanilla extract

Place pie crust in a 9" pie plate; add apples to crust and set aside. In a bowl, mix together sugar, flour and salt; stir in remaining ingredients. Beat until smooth; spoon over apples. Bake at 425 degrees for 15 minutes. Reduce oven temperature to 350 degrees. Bake for an additional 30 minutes, or until bubbly and apples are tender. Cover crust with strips of aluminum foil if crust is browning too fast. Sprinkle Crumbly Topping over pie. Bake at 400 degrees for 10 minutes, or until topping is golden. Makes 8 servings.

Crumbly Topping:

1/4 c. butter, softened
1/3 c. all-purpose flour

1/3 c. sugar
1/2 t. cinnamon

In a small bowl, mix ingredients with a fork until crumbly.

If dessert is a flop, layer it with whipped cream in a parfait glass and give it a fancy name. Nobody will know the difference!

Country Cheesecake Bars

According to Garfield, dieting is a sickness...and cheesecake is the cure! Top each bar with a spoonful of cherry pie filling for an extra-special treat.

2/3 c. butter, softened
1 c. brown sugar, packed
2 c. all-purpose flour
1 c. chopped nuts
8-oz. pkg. cream cheese,
    softened

1 c. sugar
1/4 c. milk
2 eggs, beaten
1/2 t. lemon zest
4 t. lemon juice
1 t. vanilla extract

In a bowl, mix butter, brown sugar, flour and nuts until crumbly. Set aside 2 cups of mixture for topping. Press remaining mixture into the bottom of a greased 13"x9" baking pan. Bake at 325 degrees for 15 minutes; cool. In a separate bowl, blend together remaining ingredients; pour into baked crust. Sprinkle with reserved crumb mixture. Bake for an additional 25 minutes, until set and topping is golden. Cover and refrigerate for about one hour; cut into bars. Makes 2 to 3 dozen.

Place Country Cheesecake Bars in ruffled paper muffin liners and set on a platter...so easy for everyone to serve themselves!

DINNER IS OVER... WHAT'S FOR DESSERT?

Classic Cherry Trifle

Yummy and super-easy to make ahead for a party!

8-oz. pkg. cream cheese,
    softened
3/4 c. powdered sugar
1/2 c. milk
1/3 t. vanilla extract

12-oz. container frozen whipped
    topping, thawed
1 angel food cake, cut into cubes
    and divided
2 21-oz. cans cherry pie filling

Blend together cream cheese, sugar, milk and vanilla in a bowl until smooth. Gently fold in whipped topping; set aside. In a large glass bowl, layer half of cake cubes, half of cream cheese mixture and one can pie filling. Repeat layers, ending with pie filling. Cover and refrigerate 3 to 4 hours before serving. Serves 10 to 12.

Red, White & Blueberries Trifle

It would be unpatriotic NOT to eat lots of this!

3 c. milk
5.1-oz. pkg. instant vanilla
    pudding mix
1 pound cake, cut into cubes
    and divided

12-oz. container frozen whipped
    topping, thawed
2 c. strawberries, hulled and
    sliced
1 c. blueberries

Combine milk and dry pudding mix in a bowl. Whisk for 2 minutes, until well blended. Let stand for 5 minutes, until softly set. In a large glass bowl, layer half of cake cubes, half of pudding, 1/3 of whipped topping and half each of strawberries and blueberries. Repeat layers, ending with topping. Cover and refrigerate 3 to 4 hours before serving. Serves 10 to 12.

Apple Crisp Pizza Pie

Mmm...a palate-pleasing, tastebud-teasing treat!
As if Garfield needed another reason to eat pizza!

13.8-oz. tube refrigerated
   pizza crust
2/3 c. sugar
3 T. all-purpose flour
1 t. cinnamon

4 Granny Smith apples, peeled,
   cored and sliced
1/2 c. caramel ice cream topping
Garnish: vanilla ice cream

Spread dough on a lightly greased 12" pizza pan; set aside. Combine sugar, flour and cinnamon in a large bowl; add apples and toss to coat. Arrange apple mixture in a single layer to completely cover crust. Sprinkle with Oat Topping. Bake at 350 degrees for 30 minutes, or until golden. Remove from oven; immediately drizzle with caramel topping. Cut into wedges. Serve warm, topped with a scoop of ice cream. Makes 10 to 15 servings.

Oat Topping:

1/3 c. quick-cooking oats,
   uncooked
1/2 c. all-purpose flour

1/3 c. brown sugar, packed
1 t. cinnamon
1/4 c. butter, softened

Mix together oats, flour, brown sugar and cinnamon. Stir in butter with a fork until crumbly.

Keep apple pie spice on hand to use in all kinds of desserts...even sprinkle it into hot coffee and cider. A blend of cinnamon, nutmeg and allspice, it's like a whole spice rack in a little can.

DINNER IS OVER...
WHAT'S FOR DESSERT?

Caramel Apple Cake

*Top this tender cake with a sprinkle of chopped peanuts
for a real taste of caramel apples!*

1-1/2 c. biscuit baking mix
2/3 c. sugar
1/2 c. milk
2 c. Golden Delicious apples,
    peeled, cored and sliced
1 T. lemon juice

3/4 c. brown sugar, packed
1/4 t. cinnamon
1 c. boiling water
Garnish: whipped cream,
    caramel ice cream topping

Combine biscuit mix and sugar in a bowl; stir in milk. Pour batter into
a greased 9"x9" baking pan. Arrange apples over batter; sprinkle with
lemon juice and set aside. In a separate bowl, mix brown sugar and
cinnamon; sprinkle over apples. Carefully pour water over top; do not
stir. Bake at 350 degrees for 50 minutes to one hour. Cut into squares.
Serve warm, topped with whipped cream and a drizzle of caramel
topping. Makes 4 to 6 servings.

Nothing tops real whipped cream! In a chilled bowl,
with chilled beaters, beat a cup of whipping cream on
high speed until soft peaks form. Mix in sugar and
vanilla extract to taste and enjoy!

Cherry Pie à la Mode

A classic cherry pie is made with tart pie cherries, but sweet Bing cherries may also be used. You may want to cut back on the sugar.

2 9-inch pie crusts
3 c. sour cherries, thawed
   if frozen
1 c. sugar
1/2 t. salt
1/4 c. all-purpose flour

1 T. butter
1/8 t. vanilla extract
1/8 t. almond extract
Optional: a few drops red
   food coloring
Garnish: vanilla ice cream

Place one crust in a 9" pie plate; set aside. Drain cherries, reserving juice. Measure 1/2 cup juice, adding water if necessary to equal 1/2 cup. Pour juice into a large saucepan. Whisk in sugar, salt and flour. Cook and stir over medium heat until thickened and glossy. Stir in remaining ingredients except garnish; spoon mixture into crust. Add remaining crust; flute edges and vent with a knife tip. Bake at 450 degrees for 10 minutes. Reduce oven temperature to 350 degrees. Continue baking 40 to 45 minutes, until bubbly and golden. Top each slice with a scoop of ice cream. Makes 8 servings.

Use a mini cookie cutter to cut the vents
in your pie's top crust just for fun!

DINNER IS OVER... WHAT'S FOR DESSERT?

Fresh Blueberry Pie

For a beautiful golden crust, brush a little water over the unbaked top crust and sprinkle it with sugar.

2 9-inch pie crusts
4 c. blueberries, thawed if frozen
3/4 c. sugar
3 T. cornstarch

1/2 t. cinnamon
1/8 t. salt
1 T. lemon juice
2 T. butter, sliced

Line a 9" pie plate with one crust; set aside. Place blueberries in a large bowl. In a separate bowl, combine sugar, cornstarch, cinnamon and salt; sprinkle mixture over blueberries and toss to coat. Pour blueberry mixture into crust; sprinkle with lemon juice and dot with butter. Top with remaining crust; flute edges and vent with a knife tip. Bake at 425 degrees for 30 to 40 minutes, until bubbly and crust is golden. Serves 6 to 8.

A woven lattice pie crust is impressive, but there's an easier way to make a lattice! Cut pie crust into one-inch wide strips. Place half of the strips across the pie filling in one direction, then place the remaining strips at right angles. Bake as usual.

No-Pain Blackberry Pie

*No need to pick your own berries, but this pie is
worth the trip to a thorny blackberry patch!*

2-1/2 c. blackberries, thawed
   if frozen
3 T. soft bread crumbs
3/4 c. plus 2 T. sugar, divided
1 t. cinnamon

2 T. quick-cooking tapioca,
   uncooked
8-oz. container sour cream
1/4 c. all-purpose flour

Spread blackberries evenly in an ungreased 9" pie plate; set aside. In
a small bowl, combine bread crumbs, 2 tablespoons sugar and
cinnamon. Sprinkle half the crumb mixture and all of the tapioca over
the berries. In a separate bowl, stir together sour cream, flour and
remaining sugar; spread evenly over pie. Sprinkle with remaining
crumb mixture. Bake at 375 degrees for 35 minutes, or until bubbly
and golden. Makes 8 servings.

Most fruit pies, crisps and cobblers
can be frozen up to four months. So
you can bake desserts with
ripe summer fruit, then serve
them at Thanksgiving! Cool
completely, then wrap well in
plastic wrap and two layers of
aluminum foil before freezing.
To serve, thaw overnight in the
fridge, bring to room temperature
and rewarm in the oven.

DINNER IS OVER... WHAT'S FOR DESSERT?

Blueberry Crumble

Warm and fruity with a crisp topping...dig in!

5 c. blueberries, thawed if frozen
9-inch graham cracker crust
8-oz. container sour cream
3/4 c. brown sugar, packed
3 T. all-purpose flour

1-1/2 t. vanilla extract
1/4 t. lemon zest
1/4 c. soft bread crumbs
1 T. sugar
1 T. butter, melted

Spoon blueberries into crust; set aside. In a bowl, blend together sour cream, brown sugar, flour, vanilla and lemon zest; spread evenly over blueberries. In a separate bowl, toss together remaining ingredients; sprinkle over sour cream mixture. Bake at 375 degrees for 40 minutes, or until topping is golden. Serve warm. Makes 8 servings.

Juicy fruit desserts often bubble over while baking, creating a sticky mess. A little salt poured on the spill will make it easier to clean up when the oven cools.

Homemade Applesauce

Use a combination of different kinds of apples for the most delicious applesauce. You don't even need to peel them!

6 Granny Smith apples, peeled,   1/2 c. sugar
    cored and sliced   cinnamon to taste

Place apples in a saucepan with just enough water to cover them; add sugar. Cook over medium-high heat for 10 to 15 minutes. Let cool. Mash to desired consistency. Add cinnamon to taste. Makes 4 servings.

A warm fruit compote is delightful served as a simple dessert. Simmer cut-up peaches, blueberries and raspberries together with a little honey, lemon juice and cinnamon, just until tender and syrupy. Wonderful made with fresh-picked summer fruit!

DINNER IS OVER...
WHAT'S FOR DESSERT?

Old-Fashioned Rhubarb Sauce

*A real old-time country treat. Enjoy it warm or cold,
spooned over vanilla ice cream or all by itself.*

4 c. rhubarb, trimmed and
   chopped

1/2 c. water
3/4 c. sugar

Combine all ingredients in a saucepan over medium heat. Bring to a
boil, stirring occasionally. Reduce heat to low; simmer for 10 to
12 minutes, until rhubarb is tender. Cook and stir for several more
minutes, until rhubarb breaks up and thickens slightly. Serve warm or
chilled. Serves 4 to 6.

Grab a friend and a couple of pails to visit a nearby
pick-your-own strawberry farm or peach orchard. Pretend
not to notice when your friend nibbles on the fruit
he's picked...he'll do the same for you!

Jokes

DID YOU BRING THE PAPER IN?

www.garfield.com

Distributed by Universal Press Syndicate

GARFIELD!

KIDDING! I SAVED THE FUNNIES!

Sharing

IT'S SO SAD THAT YOU DON'T KNOW HOW TO SHARE

SAD FOR YOU, MAYBE

JIM DAVIS 8-26

Do's & Don'ts for Party Hosts

- ☑ **DO** send out invites a week before your party
- ☑ **DO** plan the menu and make a shopping list
- ☑ **DO** clean out the fridge to make room for party food
- ☑ **DO** cook and freeze any make-ahead dishes
- ☑ **DO** ask a friend to help out

- 🚫 **DON'T** forget to get party supplies like forks, cups and napkins
- 🚫 **DON'T** dust and sweep 'til the day before
- 🚫 **DON'T** forget to thaw frozen party foods
- 🚫 **DON'T** put Garfield in charge of setting out the food
- 🚫 **DON'T** stress out...relax and have a great time!

Brownie Sundae Pie

Load up these ice cream-topped brownie wedges with dollops of marshmallow creme, a drizzle of chocolate sauce and all the other toppings you love...then share with friends!

1 c. sugar
1/2 c. butter, melted
2 eggs, beaten
1/2 c. all-purpose flour
1/3 c. baking cocoa

1/4 t. salt
1 t. vanilla extract
1/2 c. chopped walnuts
Garnish: vanilla ice cream,
    maraschino cherries

In a large bowl, blend together sugar and butter. Add eggs; stir well. Mix in flour, cocoa and salt; stir in vanilla and nuts. Spread in a greased and floured 9" pie plate. Bake at 350 degrees for 25 to 30 minutes, until set. Cut into wedges; serve warm, topped with scoops of ice cream and a cherry. Serves 6 to 8.

Toasting nuts adds lots of flavor...with no oil needed. Place nuts in a dry skillet over medium heat. Cook and stir until lightly golden, about 3 minutes. Cool completely before adding to recipes.

Frosty Butter Pecan Crunch Pie

Need a dessert for a summer party? This is it! One bite, and you're sure to be thinking up lots of other scrumptious ice cream & candy combinations to try.

2 c. graham cracker crumbs
1/2 c. butter, melted
2 c. milk
5.1-oz. pkg. instant vanilla
   pudding mix
2 pts. butter pecan ice cream,
   slightly softened

8-oz. container frozen whipped
   topping, thawed
2 chocolate-covered toffee candy
   bars, crushed

Toss together graham cracker crumbs and melted butter in a bowl; pat into an ungreased 13"x9" baking pan. Cover and freeze until firm, about 20 minutes. In a separate large bowl, beat together milk and dry pudding mix for 2 minutes with an electric mixer on medium speed. Fold in ice cream and whipped topping; spoon over chilled crust. Sprinkle with candy bar pieces; cover and freeze at least 2 hours. Remove from freezer 20 minutes before serving; cut into squares. Serves 12 to 15.

Do-it-yourself sandwich cookies for kids...pick up a box of graham crackers and a container of frosting. Give 'em a spatula and just turn 'em loose!

Strawberry Ice Cream Soda

Don't forget the striped straws!

1 c. frozen strawberries in
    syrup, thawed
2 pts. strawberry ice cream,
    divided

3 c. cream soda, chilled and
    divided
Garnish: whipped cream
Optional: 4 whole strawberries

In a bowl, mash strawberries in syrup until well blended. Stir together strawberries and one cup ice cream; divide into 4 tall glasses. Fill each glass with 2 tablespoons cream soda; scoop remaining ice cream equally into each glass. Slowly pour in enough soda to fill glasses. Garnish with whipped cream and a whole strawberry on the rim of each glass, if desired. Serves 4.

Soda Shoppe Root Beer Float

Frosty bottles of your favorite hometown root beer are a must!
Substitute red pop and you've just created a Pink Cow.

1 pt. vanilla ice cream
2 12-oz. bottles root beer,
    chilled

Garnish: whipped cream,
    maraschino cherries

Place one scoop ice cream into each of 4 tall glasses. Pour root beer slowly over top. Add another scoop; repeat. Garnish each glass with a dollop of whipped cream and a cherry. Serves 4.

DINNER IS OVER...
WHAT'S FOR DESSERT?

Jumpin' Java Soda

A luscious ice cream soda that's just a little bit more grown-up.
Garnish each glass with a chocolate-covered coffee bean.

1/4 c. chocolate syrup
1/4 c. half-and-half or liquid
   coffee creamer

2 pts. coffee ice cream
2 to 4 12-oz. cans cola, chilled
   and divided

In a small bowl, stir together chocolate syrup and cream or creamer.
Drizzle syrup mixture inside 4 tall glasses; add one scoop of ice cream
to each glass. Slowly pour in cola until glasses are half full. Add
remaining ice cream and cola. Serves 4.

Fill empty glass soda pop bottles with flowers,
mini American flags or pinwheels...they'll look
terrific on the picnic table!

Oodles of Snickerdoodles

These old-fashioned cookies are delicious...but mainly we just like to say snickerdoodles!

1 c. butter, softened
1-1/2 c. plus 3 T. sugar, divided
2 eggs, beaten
2-3/4 c. all-purpose flour

2 t. cream of tartar
1 t. baking soda
1/2 t. salt
2 t. cinnamon

In a large bowl, blend together butter, 1-1/2 cups sugar and eggs. Add flour, cream of tartar, baking soda and salt; mix well. Cover and chill for one hour. Combine remaining sugar and cinnamon in a small bowl. Form dough into one-inch balls; roll in sugar mixture. Arrange on ungreased baking sheets. Bake at 400 degrees for 9 to 10 minutes, until lightly golden. Let cookies cool for 2 minutes; remove to a wire rack and cool completely. Makes 3 to 4 dozen.

Magic Peanut Butter Cookies

No flour...no kidding! Presto!

1 c. creamy peanut butter
1 egg, lightly beaten

1 c. sugar
1 t. vanilla extract

Combine all ingredients in a bowl; mix well. Drop dough by teaspoonfuls onto ungreased baking sheets. Press a criss-cross pattern into each cookie with a fork. Bake at 325 degrees for 10 minutes, or until golden. Let cookies cool slightly before removing to a wire rack. Makes 2 to 3 dozen.

Sticky peanut butter or honey slides right out of
a measuring cup if you spray the cup with
non-stick vegetable spray first.

Maple-Walnut Drops

Feeling extra nutty? Press a walnut half onto
each cookie before baking.

2-1/4 c. all-purpose flour
1 t. baking soda
1 t. salt
1 c. butter, softened
3/4 c. sugar

3/4 c. brown sugar, packed
1-1/2 t. maple flavoring
2 eggs
1-1/2 c. chopped walnuts

Combine flour, baking soda and salt in a bowl; mix well and set aside. In a separate large bowl, blend butter, sugars and flavoring until creamy; beat in eggs. Gradually stir in flour mixture and walnuts. Drop dough by rounded tablespoonfuls onto ungreased baking sheets. Bake at 375 degrees for 9 to 11 minutes, until golden. Let cookies cool for several minutes; cool completely on a wire rack. Makes about 4 dozen.

Wonder why some recipes call for greased baking sheets, but some don't? Greasing the baking sheets causes cookies to spread, which for many recipes isn't desirable. If you're concerned your cookies might stick to the ungreased sheets, line baking sheets with a piece of parchment paper, which can be found near the wax paper at the grocery store.

Banana Drop Cookies

*Finally...something yummy besides banana bread
to make with extra-ripe bananas!*

2/3 c. shortening
1-3/4 c. sugar, divided
1 t. vanilla extract
2 eggs
1 c. banana, mashed

2-1/4 c. all-purpose flour
2 t. baking powder
1/4 t. salt
1 c. chopped walnuts
1/2 t. cinnamon

In a large bowl, blend shortening, 1-1/2 cups sugar and vanilla until light and fluffy. Add eggs and beat well; stir in banana. Add flour, baking powder, salt and walnuts; mix well. Cover and chill for at least 30 minutes. Drop dough by teaspoonfuls onto greased baking sheets. Mix together remaining sugar and cinnamon in a small bowl; sprinkle on unbaked cookies. Bake at 400 degrees for 8 to 10 minutes, until golden. Let cookies cool for several minutes; remove to wire racks. Makes 3 dozen.

Make sure baking powder or baking soda still has its
"oomph"...stir a teaspoonful into a mug of very hot water.
If it fizzes, it's OK to use.

DINNER IS OVER... WHAT'S FOR DESSERT?

Prize Oatmeal Cookies

A chewy, satisfying cookie...just right for a sack lunch.

1 c. butter, softened
2 c. sugar
2 eggs
2-1/2 c. all-purpose flour

1 t. baking soda
1/2 t. salt
2 c. quick-cooking oats,
  uncooked

In a large bowl, beat together butter and sugar until well blended and creamy. Add eggs; beat until light and fluffy. In a separate bowl, mix together flour, baking soda and salt. Add flour mixture to butter mixture; blend well. Stir in oats. Drop dough by teaspoonfuls onto greased baking sheets. Bake at 350 degrees for 8 to 10 minutes. Remove from oven when slightly underdone and not yet golden. Let cookies cool slightly; remove to wire racks. Makes 4 to 5 dozen.

Unless you're raisin-hating Garfield, you might enjoy adding some raisins to your Prize Oatmeal Cookies. For plump, juicy raisins, cover them with boiling water and let stand for 15 minutes. Drain raisins and pat dry with a paper towel before adding to the cookie dough.

Chewy Chocolatey Brownies

Spread with chocolate frosting...irresistible!

1 c. butter, softened
2 c. sugar
4 eggs, beaten
1 c. all-purpose flour

4 1-oz. sqs. unsweetened
    baking chocolate, melted
1 t. vanilla extract
1 c. chopped walnuts

In a bowl, blend together butter and sugar. Add eggs; mix well. Stir in remaining ingredients. Pour batter into a greased and floured 13"x9" baking pan. Bake at 350 degrees for 30 minutes. Cool; cut into squares. Makes 1-1/2 to 2 dozen.

Triple Fudgy Brownies

Try a plastic knife to cut your next pan of brownies... smooth edges all over!

2 c. milk
3.4-oz. pkg. instant chocolate
    pudding mix
18-1/2 oz. pkg. chocolate
    cake mix

1 t. vanilla extract
12-oz. pkg. semi-sweet
    chocolate chips
Garnish: powdered sugar

Combine milk and dry pudding mix in a bowl; stir just until mixture starts to thicken. Stir in dry cake mix and vanilla. Fold in chocolate chips. Spread batter in a lightly greased 13"x9" baking pan; place on center oven rack. Bake at 350 degrees for 30 to 40 minutes, until top springs back when lightly touched. Let cool at least one hour; cut into squares. Dust with powdered sugar. Makes 1-1/2 dozen.

In chocolate treats, canned pumpkin works well
as a fat-free substitute for oil.

Sneaky Zucchini Brownies

*EEK! The lady next door left a sack of zucchini
on your porch! Quick, turn 'em into brownies!*

1-1/2 c. sugar
1/2 c. oil
2 t. vanilla extract
2 c. all-purpose flour
1/2 c. baking cocoa

1 t. baking soda
1 t. salt
2 c. zucchini, shredded
1/2 c. chopped pecans

Mix sugar, oil and vanilla in a bowl; set aside. In a separate large
bowl, whisk together flour, cocoa, baking soda and salt. Blend in
sugar mixture, zucchini and pecans. Pour batter into a lightly greased
13"x9" baking pan. Bake at 350 degrees for 25 to 30 minutes, until
set. Cool; cut into squares. Makes about 1-1/2 dozen.

Peanutty Caramel Bars

*Love salty-sweet treats? Substitute dark chocolate chips
and sprinkle with a bit of kosher salt.*

14-oz. pkg. caramels,
  unwrapped
1/4 c. water
3/4 c. creamy peanut butter,
  divided

4 c. doughnut-shaped oat cereal
1 c. cocktail peanuts
1 c. milk chocolate chips
1/2 c. butter, melted

Place caramels, water and 1/2 cup peanut butter in a large saucepan.
Cook and stir over low heat until caramels are melted. Add cereal and
peanuts; stir until coated and spread in a greased 13"x9" baking pan.
In a separate saucepan over low heat, melt chocolate chips, butter and
remaining peanut butter. Spread over cereal mixture. Cover and chill;
cut into bars. Makes 2 to 3 dozen.

Chewy Chocolate Chunk Cookies

You'll want a tall glass of cold milk with these cookies!

1/2 c. butter, softened
1/2 c. brown sugar, packed
1/2 c. sugar
1 egg
1/2 t. vanilla extract
1 c. plus 2 T. all-purpose flour

1/2 t. salt
1/2 t. baking soda
1/2 c. chopped nuts
1/2 c. semi-sweet chocolate
   chunks

Blend together butter and sugars in a large bowl until creamy. Beat in egg and vanilla; set aside. In a separate bowl, combine flour, salt and baking soda; mix well and stir into butter mixture. Fold in nuts and chocolate chunks. Drop dough by teaspoonfuls onto greased baking sheets. Bake at 375 degrees for 10 minutes, or until golden. Let cookies cool slightly; cool completely on wire racks. Makes 2 dozen.

Make hand-dipped waffle cones for your favorite ice cream!
Dip the top half of waffle cones in melted chocolate chips,
then roll them in candy sprinkles or chopped nuts.

DINNER IS OVER...
WHAT'S FOR DESSERT?

Indoor S'mores

*Don't let a rainy day spoil your picnic plans! Enjoy the
great indoors by whipping up a pan of these
chocolatey treats...no campfire needed.*

12 whole graham crackers
1/4 c. butter
16-oz. pkg. marshmallows

12-oz. pkg. semi-sweet
chocolate chips
1 c. chopped peanuts

Line a 15"x10" jelly-roll pan with aluminum foil, extending foil over
edges of pan. Spray with non-stick vegetable spray. Arrange graham
crackers in pan in a single layer; set aside. Melt butter in a large
saucepan over low heat. Add marshmallows; stir constantly until
melted. Place chocolate chips in a microwave-safe bowl; cook on high
setting for 2 to 3 minutes, stirring every 30 seconds, until melted. Add
chocolate to marshmallow mixture. Stir to blend; immediately pour
onto graham crackers and spread to edges. Sprinkle with peanuts. Cool
until set, refrigerating if desired. Lift bars out of pan by aluminum foil
"handles." Cut into squares with a pizza cutter. Makes 2 dozen.

Stoke up a fire in the fireplace for a casual fireside
supper. Toast sandwiches in pie irons and make s'mores
over the fire for dessert...so cozy!

Monster Cookies

Makes a monstrously large batch of delicious cookies.
Indulge, then join Garfield for a monster nap!

6 eggs, beaten
1 c. butter
16-oz. pkg. brown sugar
2 c. sugar
2 T. vanilla extract
6 T. light corn syrup
3 c. creamy peanut butter

4 t. baking soda
9 c. quick-cooking oats,
  uncooked
1-1/2 c. semi-sweet chocolate
  chips
1-1/2 c. peanuts
1-1/2 c. candy-coated chocolates

In a very large bowl, mix all ingredients in the order listed. Drop dough
by rounded teaspoonfuls onto ungreased baking sheets. Bake at
350 degrees for 12 to 16 minutes, until golden. Let cookies cool for
several minutes. Remove from baking sheets to wire racks and cool
completely. Makes 10 to 12 dozen.

WANT COOKIES.
COOKIES GOOD

For the best results when
baking a large batch, don't
overcrowd the oven! Bake just
two baking sheets of cookies
at a time. Halfway through
the baking time, swap the
pans between oven racks...
your cookies will be
perfectly baked.

Giant Chocolate Chip Cookies

Mmm...the cookies of Jon and Garfield's dreams!

2 c. all-purpose flour
1/2 t. baking soda
1/2 t. salt
3/4 c. butter, melted
1 c. brown sugar, packed
1/2 c. sugar

1 egg
1 egg yolk
1 T. vanilla extract
12-oz. pkg. semi-sweet
   chocolate chips

In a bowl, combine flour, baking soda and salt; mix well and set aside. In a separate large bowl, beat together butter and sugars until well blended. Add egg, egg yolk and vanilla; beat until light and creamy. Add flour mixture to butter mixture; stir until just blended. Stir in chocolate chips. Form dough into balls by 1/4 cupfuls. Place on greased or parchment paper-lined baking sheets, 2 inches apart. Bake at 325 degrees for 15 to 17 minutes, until edges are golden. Cool cookies on baking sheets for several minutes; remove to wire racks. Makes about 15 cookies.

Homemade ice cream sandwiches! Spread softened ice cream on one cookie and top with another cookie. Roll edges of ice cream in chocolate sprinkles or crushed peppermint candies, wrap with plastic wrap and freeze until solid.

Applesauce Spice Bars

*In a hurry? Frost these moist, spicy bars with creamy
ready-to-use caramel or vanilla frosting.*

1 c. all-purpose flour
2/3 c. brown sugar, packed
1 t. baking soda
1/2 t. salt
1 t. apple pie spice

1/4 c. shortening
1 egg, beaten
1 c. applesauce
1 c. chopped walnuts or raisins

Combine all ingredients in a large bowl; mix thoroughly. Spread batter
in a greased 13"x9" baking pan. Bake at 350 degrees for about
25 minutes, until set. Let cool; frost with Browned Butter Frosting.
Cut into small bars. Makes 2-1/2 to 3 dozen.

Browned Butter Frosting:

3 T. butter
1-1/2 c. powdered sugar

1 t. vanilla extract
1 to 1-1/2 T. milk

Heat butter in a saucepan over medium heat until it turns a light
golden brown; remove from heat. Stir in remaining ingredients. Beat
until frosting is smooth and spreadable.

Make clean-up a snap! Before you start baking, fill the sink
with hot, soapy water. Toss in mixing bowls and utensils as
soon as you finish using them. They'll be a breeze to wash by
the time the last pan of cookies is pulled from the oven.

DINNER IS OVER...
WHAT'S FOR DESSERT?

Soft Pumpkin Cookies

*For Halloween fun, frost these cookies with orange frosting,
then use candies to create Jack-o'-Lantern faces.
Remember, a treat in your mouth is worth two in the bag!*

2-1/2 c. all-purpose flour
1 t. baking powder
1 t. baking soda
1-1/2 t. cinnamon
1/2 t. salt

1/2 c. butter, softened
1-1/2 c. sugar
1 c. canned pumpkin
1 egg, beaten
1 t. vanilla extract

In a large bowl, combine flour, baking powder, baking soda, cinnamon and salt. In a separate bowl, beat together butter and sugar in a separate bowl until blended. Stir in pumpkin, egg and vanilla until smooth. Gradually add flour mixture to butter mixture; stir well. Drop dough by rounded tablespoonfuls onto greased baking sheets. Bake at 350 degrees for 15 to 18 minutes, until edges are firm. Cool cookies on baking sheets for 2 minutes; transfer to a wire rack. Cool completely; drizzle with Powdered Sugar Glaze. Makes about 2 dozen.

Powdered Sugar Glaze:

2 c. powdered sugar
3 T. milk

1 T. butter, melted
1 t. vanilla extract

Combine ingredients in a small bowl; mix until smooth.

Whole-wheat pastry flour
is ideal for making your
favorite cookie recipe a
little healthier. Substitute
it for some or all of
the all-purpose flour
in the recipe.

Sugar Cookie Cut-Outs

You'll use this recipe year 'round to make Valentine hearts, Easter eggs, Halloween pumpkins and, of course, Christmas cookies!

1 c. butter, softened
1 c. sugar
1 t. vanilla or almond extract
1 egg, beaten

2 t. baking powder
3 c. all-purpose flour
Garnish: frosting, candy
　　sprinkles

In a large bowl, blend together butter and sugar; stir in vanilla and egg. In a separate bowl, mix baking powder and flour. Add flour mixture to butter mixture, one cup at a time, blending well. Roll out dough on a floured surface, 1/8-inch thick. Cut out dough with cookie cutters. Place cookies on ungreased baking sheets. Bake at 400 degrees for 6 to 7 minutes, until lightly golden. Cool cookies on a wire rack. Frost and decorate as desired. Makes about 2 dozen.

A simple trick for perfectly shaped cut-out cookies! Place cookies on parchment-paper lined baking sheets. Pop them in the fridge for 15 minutes or so, until firm, then bake as usual.

DINNER IS OVER...
WHAT'S FOR DESSERT?

Easy Gingerbread Men

Santa's favorite cookies...and Garfield loves 'em too!

18-1/2 oz. pkg. spice cake mix
1 c. all-purpose flour
2 t. ground ginger
2 eggs

1/3 c. oil
1/2 c. light molasses
Garnish: frosting, candy
    sprinkles, small candies

Place dry cake mix, flour and ginger in a large bowl; stir until blended. Stir in remaining ingredients except garnish. Beat with an electric mixer on medium speed for 2 minutes. Cover dough and refrigerate for 2 hours. Roll out dough on a floured surface, 1/4-inch thick. Cut out dough with cookie cutters. Place cookies on greased baking sheets. Bake at 375 degrees for 8 to 10 minutes, until edges start to darken. Let cookies cool on baking sheets for 5 minutes; cool on wire racks. Frost and decorate as desired. Makes 2 to 3 dozen.

It's fun to decorate cookies with friends! Set out lots of cookies along with tubes of frosting, sparkly sugar, candy sprinkles and mini candies, and just let everyone go wild. Be sure to have extras for nibbling, plus a pitcher of icy cold milk to serve when you sample your cookie creations!

Fruit Cookie Gems

These fruit-filled cookies might change your mind about fruitcake!
It's fine to mix & match fruit too. You can use all candied cherries
or pineapple instead of mixed fruit as long as you use 2 cups.

1/2 c. shortening
1-1/2 c. brown sugar, packed
2 eggs
2 c. all-purpose flour
1/2 t. baking soda
1/2 t. salt
1 t. cinnamon

1/4 t. ground cloves
2 c. mixed candied fruit, diced
2 c. golden raisins
Optional: 1-1/2 c. chopped
   walnuts
1/2 c. evaporated milk
2 t. white vinegar

Blend together shortening and brown sugar in a large bowl; beat in
eggs. In a separate bowl, combine flour, baking soda, salt and spices;
mix well. Stir in raisins, fruit and nuts, if using. Add to shortening
mixture along with milk and vinegar; mix well. Drop dough by
teaspoonfuls onto greased baking sheets. Bake at 325 degrees for
20 to 25 minutes, until set and golden. Cool cookies on wire racks.
Makes about 6 dozen.

Cheer up a friend in a jiffy. Wrap up several homemade
cookies in plastic wrap and tie with a bow. Tuck them into a
big coffee mug along with a packet of gourmet coffee, then
sneak them onto your friend's porch or desk as a surprise.

DINNER IS OVER...
WHAT'S FOR DESSERT?

Molasses Crinkles

An old farm favorite...perfect with a cup of coffee.

3/4 c. shortening
1 c. brown sugar, packed
1 egg, beaten
1/4 c. light molasses
2-1/4 c. all-purpose flour

1/4 t. baking soda
1 t. cinnamon
1 t. ground ginger
Garnish: sugar

In a large bowl, mix together shortening, brown sugar, egg and molasses. Stir in remaining ingredients except garnish in order listed. Roll dough into one-inch balls. Dip tops in sugar and place on ungreased baking sheets. Gently press a thumbprint into each. Sprinkle one to 4 drops of water in each indentation. Bake at 350 degrees for 10 to 12 minutes, until golden. Let cookies cool on wire racks. Makes 4 dozen.

Fizzy Milk Punch

A refreshing and easy-to-make party punch.

1/2 c. water
1 c. sugar
5-oz. can evaporated milk

3 2-ltr. bottles lemon-lime soda, chilled
1/2 to 1 gal. vanilla ice cream

In a saucepan, combine water and sugar. Cook and stir over medium heat until sugar is dissolved. Remove from heat; stir in milk. Let cool; cover and refrigerate. Just before serving, combine chilled milk mixture and lemon-lime soda in a punch bowl. Add as many scoops of ice cream as desired.
Serves 18 to 24.

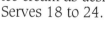

Candy Cane Snowballs

For extra-frosty snowballs, add some sparkly white decorator sugar to the candy mixture.

1/2 c. peppermint candy, finely crushed and divided
1/4 c. plus 1/3 c. powdered sugar, divided
1 c. butter, softened
1 t. vanilla extract
2-1/4 c. all-purpose flour
1/4 t. salt

Combine 1/4 cup crushed candy and 1/4 cup powdered sugar in a shallow bowl; set aside. In a separate large bowl, combine butter, remaining candy, remaining powdered sugar and vanilla. Beat together with an electric mixer on medium speed. Stir in flour and salt. Form into one-inch balls; place on ungreased baking sheets. Bake at 325 degrees for 12 to 15 minutes, until set but not browned. Immediately remove cookies from baking sheets; roll in candy mixture. Place cookies on a wire rack. Roll again in candy mixture when cooled completely. Makes about 2-1/2 dozen.

To crush peppermint candy for Candy Cane Snowballs, place the candy in a large plastic zipping bag. Tap it gently with a kitchen mallet until the candy is broken up. It's tasty sprinkled on frosted cupcakes too.

DINNER IS OVER...
WHAT'S FOR DESSERT?

Odie's Peppermint Bark

So easy to make...wrap some up for Christmas gifts!

2 12-oz. pkgs. white chocolate
chips
1 t. peppermint extract

1/2 c. peppermint candy,
crushed

In a microwave-safe bowl, microwave chocolate chips on high setting for 30 seconds; stir. Microwave for another 30 seconds. Stir in extract and crushed candy. Spread onto a parchment paper-lined baking sheet. Cover loosely and refrigerate for 2 hours; break into pieces. Store in an airtight container. Makes about 1-1/2 pounds.

Never-Fail Divinity Candy

Mom's tried & true advice: always choose a sunny, clear day to make candy! Rainy or humid weather can make it flop.

7-oz. jar marshmallow creme
1/2 c. water
2 c. sugar

1/8 t. salt
Optional: 1/4 c. chopped pecans

Spoon marshmallow creme into a large heat-proof bowl; set aside. Combine water, sugar and salt in a saucepan over medium-high heat. Bring to a rolling boil; boil and stir for 2 minutes. Pour hot mixture over marshmallow creme. Stir until well blended and mixture loses its gloss. Stir in pecans, if using. Drop by teaspoonfuls onto wax paper-lined baking sheets; let stand several hours until dry. Store in an airtight container. Makes about 1-1/2 pounds.

Double-the-Fun Fudge

So much more delicious than the fudge you get at the state fair!
This recipe will go more quickly if you can line up a stirring helper.

1 c. peanut butter chips
1 c. semi-sweet chocolate chips
2-1/4 c. sugar
5-oz. can evaporated milk

1/4 c. butter
7-oz. jar marshmallow creme
1-1/4 t. vanilla extract

Place peanut butter chips in a large bowl; place chocolate chips in a separate large bowl. Line an 8"x8" pan with aluminum foil, extending foil over edges of pan. Spray with non-stick vegetable spray; set aside. In a heavy saucepan over medium heat, combine sugar, milk, butter and marshmallow creme. Stirring constantly, bring to a rolling boil. Boil and stir for 5 minutes. Remove saucepan from heat; stir in vanilla. Immediately pour half of hot mixture onto peanut butter chips. Stir until smooth; pour into prepared pan. Quickly add remaining hot mixture to chocolate chips. Stir until smooth; pour into pan. Cover and refrigerate until cooled completely, one to 2 hours. Use the edges of foil as handles to remove fudge from pan. Turn fudge onto a cutting board and peel off foil. Cut into small squares. Store in an airtight container. Makes about 2 pounds.

Take-out containers are just right for packing gifts of fudge or cookies. You'll find them at craft stores in a rainbow of colors.

INDEX

INDEX

INDEX

Have a taste for more?

We created our official Circle of Friends so we could fill everyone in on the latest scoop at once. Visit us online to join in the fun and discover free recipes, exclusive giveaways and much more!

www.gooseberrypatch.com

Call us toll-free at 1·800·854·6673

U.S. to Canadian recipe equivalents

Volume Measurements

1/4 teaspoon	1 mL
1/2 teaspoon	2 mL
1 teaspoon	5 mL
1 tablespoon = 3 teaspoons	15 mL
2 tablespoons = 1 fluid ounce	30 mL
1/4 cup	60 mL
1/3 cup	75 mL
1/2 cup = 4 fluid ounces	125 mL
1 cup = 8 fluid ounces	250 mL
2 cups = 1 pint =16 fluid ounces	500 mL
4 cups = 1 quart	1 L

Weights

1 ounce	30 g
4 ounces	120 g
8 ounces	225 g
16 ounces = 1 pound	450 g

Oven Temperatures

300° F	150° C
325° F	160° C
350° F	180° C
375° F	190° C
400° F	200° C
450° F	230° C

Baking Pan Sizes

Square

8x8x2 inches	2 L = 20x20x5 cm
9x9x2 inches	2.5 L = 23x23x5 cm

Rectangular

13x9x2 inches	3.5 L = 33x23x5 cm

Loaf

9x5x3 inches	2 L = 23x13x7 cm

Round

8x1-1/2 inches	1.2 L = 20x4 cm
9x1-1/2 inches	1.5 L = 23x4 cm